A Home for Wayward Boys

A HOME FOR WAYWARD BOYS

*The Early History of the
Alabama Boys' Industrial School*

JERRY C. ARMOR

NEWSOUTH BOOKS

Montgomery

NewSouth Books
105 S. Court Street
Montgomery, AL 36104

Copyright © 2015 by Jerry C. Armor
All rights reserved under International and Pan-American Copyright Conventions. Published in the United States by NewSouth Books, a division of NewSouth, Inc., Montgomery, Alabama.

Library of Congress Cataloging-in-Publication Data

Armor, Jerry C.
A home for wayward boys : the early history of the Alabama Boys' Industrial School / Jerry C. Armor.
pages cm
Includes bibliographical references and index.

ISBN 978-1-60306-345-6 (paperback) — ISBN 978-1-60306-378-4 (ebook)

1. Alabama Boys' Industrial School. 2. Reformatories—Alabama—History. 3. Juvenile delinquents—Rehabilitation—Alabama—History. 4. Juvenile delinquents—Education—Alabama—History. I. Title.
HV9105.A3A76 2014
365'.42—dc23
2014035913

SOURCES OF ILLUSTRATIONS

Grateful appreciation is expressed to the following providers of the photographs and documents appearing in this work:
Pages 6, 36, 126, 128: Birmingham Printing and Publishing, Inc.
Pages 17, 22, 23, 44, 48–51, 60, 65, 81, 86, 91, 94–95, 99, 103, 106, 118, 122, 135–137: Alabama Department of Archives and History, Montgomery, Alabama.
Pages 28, 67–70, 92, 101, 116, 141–142, 150: Scott Dawsey.
Pages 127, 155–156, 159–162: Alabama Department of Youth Services.
Pages 148, 152: Birmingham, Ala. Public Library Archives, Portrait Collection.

Design by Randall Williams
Printed in the United States of America

To my wife, Judy,
and my mother, Racine

Contents

Foreword / ix
Preface / xi

1. I Have the Jawbone / 3
2. It Was God's Work / 10
3. A Mother's Love / 16
4. Building on Faith / 21
5. The Start Is Made / 27
6. Spurgeon and Other Headaches / 34
7. We Had to Go / 42
8. Dwelling in Green Pastures / 47
9. An Open Door / 57
10. An Honest Trade / 63
11. The Junk Heap / 75
12. Down on the Farm / 80
13. Training Heart, Head, and Hands / 86
14. Present Arms! / 91
15. Blowing a Horn / 98
16. The Boys' Banner / 107
17. A Winning Reputation / 117
18. Amen / 124
19. Healing Body and Soul / 131
20. Boys Will Be Boys / 139
21. End of an Era / 146
22. Change / 154

Epilogue / 164
Notes / 171
Bibliography / 178
Index / 182

Foreword

Wayne Flynt

Failure of political vision and leadership has been both a tragedy and an opportunity for Alabamians: tragedy in that so many opportunities to advance progress and justice have been delayed or lost entirely; opportunity in that when leaders fail, ordinary citizens either have to reconcile themselves to conditions they consider unconscionable or change them. In the case of Elizabeth Johnston, she vowed to challenge injustice. A club woman and deeply religious, married to a prominent bank president and the sister-in-law to a governor, she had just the right combination of moral compass, organizing ability, and circle of influential friends to transform the way in which troubled (white) boys were treated in the state.

As volunteer Sunday School teacher for a decade in the prison camp operated by Pratt Coal Company north of Birmingham, she was appalled at the age of some child convicts (some as young as 14). Believing that all children, even wayward ones, deserved love, attention, decent housing, food, education, and opportunity to learn a trade, Johnston began to lobby her powerful friends to establish a boys' industrial school. She first mobilized the newly created Alabama Federation of Women's Clubs, then her larger circle of business and political leaders, always willing to do the dirty work of lobbying and carefully expending the resources obtained from them.

Reading about this remarkable woman, her passionate desire to help boys that others abandoned, her self-education as a construction manager, her indefatigable energy, is enough to inspire the reader. But there is a much larger cast of actors in this drama: social workers and ministers; club women; prison reformers; the first (and barely trained) superintendents of the school, learning as they administered; and the boys, learning to believe in themselves because so many influential adults believed in them. Whether the reader is captivated by the skilled craftsmen some of the boys became, the band they formed, the impressive record of their service in World War II, or merely the responsible lives so many graduates lived, every reader will be informed about an institution which demonstrates the limitless possibilities of the human spirit.

This is a book about a little-known subject that will amaze, inform, and inspire the reader.

Wayne Flynt taught more than 6,000 students, mainly at Samford and Auburn universities, during a 40-year teaching career. He also authored or co-authored 13 books, primarily about Alabama.

Preface

I first became acquainted with the Alabama Boys' Industrial School in early 1975, long after the heydays of Elizabeth Johnston and David Weakley. I had just graduated from Samford University in Birmingham with a degree in history and Spanish and returned to my hometown of Moulton, Alabama, to await entrance to graduate school at the University of Alabama in the fall. It was my intention to earn a master's degree in Latin American Studies and follow in the footsteps of mentors like Drs. Wayne Flynt and Myralyn Allgood in becoming a college professor.

As I awaited the fall, things changed. The local juvenile court judge, the Honorable Cecil Caine Jr., asked if I would consider being our county's first juvenile probation officer. Alabama was revamping its juvenile court system and establishing juvenile probation officers in every county, thus removing that function from the State Department of Pensions and Security. The invitation caught me off guard; I didn't know what a juvenile probation officer was, much less have any desire to be one. The position was funded by a grant, making its future somewhat uncertain, and the pay was less than attractive. For some unknown reason, however, I was intrigued. I thought—at the very least—that I could take the job for a few months, make a little spending money, and then resign in about eight months when the fall term began.

A funny thing happened—I began to enjoy the work. I discovered that it had many of the same rewards I was seeking as a college professor, primarily the opportunity to have an impact on young people's lives. When the fall semester arrived, I turned down the opportunity at the University of Alabama and remained with the juvenile court.

So it was that I was introduced to the Alabama Boys' Industrial School.

One of my first clients, I soon learned, was actually AWOL—an escapee—from the school. When he was finally captured by the county sheriff's department, it was my responsibility to accompany a deputy in returning the boy to the school. Though the school was no longer the pristine campus of its earlier days, it still had a certain grace and beauty, like an aging socialite. The buildings were impressive, if badly in need of repair. Mature trees dotted a lush but unkempt campus. Everything looked like it could use a good cleaning. I gave all that little thought. As a twenty-two-year-old juvenile probation officer, I was more concerned about keeping my young clients on the straight and narrow than the condition of this, my first reform school. I made numerous trips to the school over the next seven years, never bothering to look much beyond the deteriorating facade of the campus.

As the years went by, some aspects of the job began to wear on me, especially the rigors of constantly being on call during evenings and weekends. I had earned a master's degree in correctional counseling during this time, and my thoughts returned to the notion of teaching in college, but this time in the field of criminal justice. I got that opportunity in 1981 and began a career that to this point has spanned thirty years, primarily at Calhoun Community College and Athens State University. Along the way, I finally kept that appointment at the University of Alabama, where I completed my doctorate.

Only in the last few years was I reminded of the Alabama Boys' Industrial School. I was doing some research for one of my classes and went to the website of the Alabama Department of Archives and History. When I ran across a number of photos from the institution's earliest years, my fascination with the state's first juvenile reformatory was rekindled. With more digging, I discovered the affectionate biography of Elizabeth Johnston, the visionary founder; I stumbled upon a handwritten diary of the first superintendent, C. D. Griffin; and I found the papers left behind by David Weakley, the longtime heart and soul of the school. Just as significant, I learned that no one had ever written a comprehensive work on the distinctive old school.

I thoroughly enjoyed the research and writing of this project. Each new day brought a new revelation about this school I thought I knew. How did a boys' institution in the late 1800s end up with a female board of directors? Who ever heard of a reform school with a marching band? Who knew that an institution for juvenile offenders provided military training for its residents, or had a student newspaper? It certainly wasn't anything like I had ever encountered in studying and visiting present-day juvenile reformatories. To put it simply, the whole place exuded a charm and quaintness that made it very appealing.

Things were not as idyllic, however, for the black youth of Alabama who remained confined in the adult penal system. Because of the political and social climate of the South at the time, Mrs. Johnston's new school would be for whites only. To say that Mrs. Johnston condoned this segregation would be unfair. On the contrary, there is evidence in this book that she had an open heart toward people of color, and likely would have also opened the doors to her school had the opportunity presented itself. Thankfully, leaders in Alabama's African American community came to the rescue of their own children in 1911 when a similar school for black boys was started in Mt. Meigs. Although the Alabama Industrial School for Negro Children began with much promise, conditions there eventually deteriorated until they were no better than the adult prison camps. The situation would not improve until all three of Alabama's reform schools were integrated and brought under the control of the Alabama Department of Youth Services in the 1970s.

I hope you will find the Alabama Boys' Industrial School as fascinating as I have. Whatever has motivated you to open this book, it is my hope that you, too, will be captivated by this school for wayward boys and its leaders dedicated to turning them into men.

Acknowledgments

This project would not have been possible without the assistance, support and encouragement of many people.

The Alabama Department of Archives and History and the Archives at the Birmingham Public Library were most gracious and helpful in allowing me access to numerous government documents and the papers of C. D. Griffin and David Weakley.

Arthur Henley of Birmingham Printing and Publishing allowed me to use photographs and source material from Mary Avery Johnston's rare biography of her beloved aunt.

Scott Dawsey shared with me the photographs and stories of his grandfather, James Dawsey. It has been a pleasure to make a new friend of someone who appreciates the history of the Alabama Boys' Industrial School (ABIS).

James Thomas and his staff at the Alabama Department of Youth Services (ADYS) Vacca Campus welcomed me to their facility on several occasions to view documents and conduct interviews. Having worked with juvenile offenders myself, I have the utmost respect for the work you do and the challenges you face.

Longtime friend Allen Peaton at the ADYS administrative offices provided valuable statistics and photographs of the campus.

My colleagues and the administration at Athens State University gave me the support necessary to balance this project with my other duties and responsibilities.

Former professor and mentor Dr. Wayne Flynt—himself once a college volunteer at ABIS—read the manuscript and offered invaluable suggestions. I am relieved he did not put as many red notations in the margins as he did on my exams at Samford.

My cousin Sonny Bass gave much of his time preparing my photographs for publication and serving as a traveling companion on numerous trips to Montgomery.

Randall Williams, Suzanne La Rosa, Jeff Benton, Brian Seidman, Sam Robards, McCormick Williams, Lisa Harrison, Blair Johnson, Ashley Stanaland and other staff at NewSouth Books made my first efforts at publishing a book a great experience. Let's do it again sometime.

Finally, thanks to my mother, Mrs. Curtis Armor, for giving me a love of books and gentling nudging me toward the finish line, and to my wife, Judy, for her love, patience, and assistance in so many ways. Maybe one day we will find out what happened to Spurgeon.

A Home for Wayward Boys

1

I Have the Jawbone

Determination evident in her face, the little girl trudged across the plowed field with an entourage of children trailing behind. Johnsie Evans was taking the first steps in what would turn out to be a lifelong quest for the betterment of those less fortunate than herself. That pursuit would eventually lead to the establishment of one of the nation's premier schools for wayward boys.

From her early childhood, it was evident that Elizabeth Johnson Evans was special. Using the personal traits bestowed upon her at birth along with those developed during her remarkable life, she was destined for greatness. For Johnsie, that meant a life devoted to serving her Lord and her fellow man.

The little girl, dubbed "Johnsie" by her father, was born to Peter and Lizzie Morehead Evans of North Carolina in May 1851. The best novelist could not imagine a more romanticized Old South life than the one Johnsie's family lived. Although history has taught that the Evanses' lifestyle was not the norm, theirs appears to be one case where fact lived up to fiction. As one writer put it, she was "born to the purple."[1] Her maternal grandfather was the governor of North Carolina. Both of her parents had grown up on sprawling plantations with slaves to do their bidding. It is said that during their courtship, Peter would send a messenger on a three-day ride just to deliver his love letters to Lizzie. Beechwood, the plantation house where Johnsie grew up, was elegantly furnished and decorated.

This was definitely Southern aristocracy at its grandest, with one major caveat. Despite the affluence in which they lived, Johnsie's parents seem to have been well-grounded. They instilled Christian character and values into their daughter. It does appear that Peter Evans was a benevolent slavemaster, providing his charges with brick cottages replete with glass windowpanes, a point that became a source of pride for the inhabitants.

Johnsie noted that her father was "as kind as he was strict" to his hundreds of slaves. Mrs. Evans supervised the women involved in domestic labor such as weaving and sewing, while also providing a nursery and Sunday worship services.[2]

So, while the Evanses enjoyed the fruits of the slavery system, within it they appear to have tried to live up to the biblical admonition that "to whom much is given, much is required." They seemed to take seriously their obligation to help the less fortunate. In sharing her life story with her niece, Johnsie related this lesson and many others she learned from her parents and through her childhood experiences. These lessons proved instrumental in providing the motivation and skills she needed to establish a school for wayward boys years later.

Johnsie would no doubt profess that the most important principle that sustained her throughout her marvelous journey was her unwavering faith in God. That seed was planted early in Johnsie's life. In fact, she often said that an incident illustrating Jesus's abiding presence was her earliest childhood memory.

Johnsie and her parents were on an overnight visit at a relative's home. At bedtime, Johnsie realized that this would be her first night to sleep in a room apart from her parents. Fears flooded her mind and filled her with dread. She began to cry and begged her mother not to leave her alone.

"What do you fear my child?" her mother consoled her. "Jesus is with you here as well as anywhere."

Temporarily pacified, Johnsie drifted off to sleep, only to be awakened by the nightmare of a man being in the room. She started to scream as her fears returned in full force. But suddenly she remembered her mother's comforting words that "Jesus is with you."

"Dear Jesus," the little girl spoke aloud, "just put your hand on my head and take care of me." With her assurance renewed, she drifted back to sleep. For years afterward, it was always her testimony that his comforting "hand" was never far away when she needed it.[3]

That childlike trust and dependence would remain an integral part of Johnsie's life. Many marveled during her lifetime at her conversational relationship with her Heavenly Father. That relationship carried her during the tragedies in her personal life and the trials she encountered in her service to others.

The desire to serve the less fortunate took root early in Johnsie's life. One day she was weeding in the garden when a group of slave children ran urgently up to her. "Lil' Miss, that overseer is plowing up us colored folks' graveyard," one shouted breathlessly. Immediately, the master's daughter dropped her tools and started across the plowed field toward the cemetery.

"Stop! Stop!" she called to the foreman. "Don't you dare plow up one of those graves," she called out in the most authoritative voice that such a child could muster. "If you touch one of them I will have my father turn you off at once."[4]

She then gave all of those present an impassioned speech on a person's obligation to look out for one's neighbors. The lesson must have taken hold, for the overseer decided to find fertile ground elsewhere. This episode was the first of many persuasive speeches that Johnsie would be called upon to deliver on behalf of others to governors, legislators, businessmen, and civic groups.

It was about that same time that the young girl, now about eight, learned a thing or two about financial responsibility and the burden of debt. For some time, she had longed for a "store-bought" doll from New York, with "real hair" and eyes that "open and shut." And the price for such a treasure was "only six dollars."

In the antebellum South, six dollars was no small consideration. She thought several times about approaching her father to ask for the doll, but lost her nerve each time. Finally, she settled on writing him a note asking if he would loan her the necessary money. It was her notion that he would be touched by her request and buy her the doll as a gift. She miscalculated. Instead, he agreed to her proposition upon the explicit condition that she repay him in full.

When the doll arrived from New York some weeks later, she was overjoyed. In her exuberance, she exclaimed, "I will never do anything but dress and undress my precious doll, put her to sleep and wake her up." A demanding look from her father quickly reminded the child of her agreement. She was allowed one free day to play with her new companion before she was

A youthful Elizabeth "Johnsie" Evans displays some of the "ineffable darlingness" that won the heart of General Robert Johnston.

placed on a strict routine of cleaning her room, picking cotton, or whatever chore her father thought was appropriate for the day. Only the beginning of the hostilities between the North and South interrupted Johnsie's payment schedule. [5]

The Civil War disrupted Johnsie's life in a much more significant way. Her father, always a horseman, enlisted in the 64th North Carolina Cavalry and rose to the rank of colonel in the Confederate Army. In May of 1863, Johnsie and her mother were allowed to visit Colonel Evans at his encampment. As she recalled years later, it was a bittersweet reunion in that it was the last time she ever saw her father. The following month, Evans was wounded in a battle in Virginia and taken to a prison camp near Washington, D.C. Now twelve years old, the adventurous Johnsie and a male cousin secretly made plans to run away from home to see Evans at the prison hospital. As the date of their mission neared, the family received word that Evans had succumbed to his wounds.

The indelible image of her father dying as a prisoner of war left a lasting mark on the girl. As she thought about the agony he suffered and the horrible conditions he endured in his last days, she felt herself being called to help those who were incarcerated. Although it would be years before that premonition would become a reality, it set her on a course from which she would never waver. [6]

As little Johnsie turned into an adolescent Miss Evans, it became apparent that another quality she had in abundance was charm. One of her many admirers described it in one of his love letters as "ineffable darlingness." There were many suitors. The story is told of a trip to Morgantown she made as a young lady of eighteen years. While staying in one of the city's finest hotels, a number of callers came to make her acquaintance while she was in town. One was named Robert Bingham.

"Well, I warrant you are here to see Miss Johnsie Evans," the clerk at the desk surmised as he peered over his glasses at Bingham. "Well, my young boy, you are the ninth that has come, but each of you will go away happier for just seeing her."

In a fitting conclusion to this story, the same Robert Bingham's grandson had the pleasure of meeting the lovely lady some sixty-five years later.

The courteous young gentleman bowed and kissed her hand.

"Madam, I am the tenth," he said to the still beautiful woman, now in her eighties.

"Would I were younger, or you older, Bob Bingham's grandson!" she quickly replied. [7]

Such charm would be indispensable as she begged, pleaded, cajoled, and humored those around her into helping those she would lovingly refer to as "her boys."

The suitor who ultimately won her heart was former Confederate General Robert Douglas Johnston. Sixteen years her senior, General Johnston had to wage quite a campaign before Johnsie finally agreed to marriage. She told her niece that he proposed "exactly thirty-six times" before she finally told him, "Well, I suppose I will have to do it in order to get rid of you." [8]

After marrying, the couple moved into a home that adjoined the Johnston family property in Charlotte, North Carolina. Their life together there was full and vibrant. They were active in their church, as well as the civic and social scene of the community. Two years into their marriage they were blessed with the first of their eight children. [9]

As idyllic as their life was, there were still obstacles. However with her indomitable spirit, these hardships only steeled Johnsie for the tasks that lay ahead. The first of these concerned her health. When Johnsie was just a child, a diphtheria epidemic left her with diminished hearing and also claimed the life of her younger sister. Her hearing got progressively worse with time. During the first years of her marriage, General Johnston took his wife to New York to a specialist, but to no avail.[10] She would have to contend with this challenge the rest of her life. Ultimately Johnsie came to believe that this deficiency made her more sensitive in other ways. The 1944 biography by her niece, Mary Johnston Avery, is entitled *She Heard with Her Heart* in recognition of her facility for communicating with those who were hurting. Describe it as empathy, compassion, or any number of other terms, but Johnsie seemed to have the ability to sense what others were feeling in their hearts.[11]

The scourge of diphtheria again touched Johnsie's life years later when the awful disease ravaged Charlotte. One of its many victims was the Johnstons' oldest child, Louise. The young mother was deeply affected, but instead of turning inward, she looked outward to the plight of others. She became aware of the need for a hospital in Charlotte to serve the black community and threw her energy into that effort. However, her commitment to that endeavor did not come until after she had one of those famous conversations with her Lord.

"O, Lord, why did you start me at this," she pleaded. "You know I have no money to build a hospital myself, and lack the ability to make others see the need!"

"I slew a thousand Philistines with the jaw-bone of an ass," she seemed to hear him say.

"All right then, I have the jaw-bone!" she replied with a laugh.[12]

With her determination and hard work, and the Lord's guidance and provision, the black hospital became a reality. Little did she realize that this contribution to Charlotte would be her last. The Lord was calling her family to a new venue and Johnsie to a new venture.

Building the hospital was a worthy cause and definitely met a need in Charlotte. At the same time it was an ideal proving ground for the skills that Johnsie would need for a much larger initiative she would champion just a few years later.

2

It Was God's Work

In 1890, Johnsie Johnston was called to the mission field. No, it was not in the traditional sense of the word. She would not be preaching to natives on foreign soil, but she would definitely be on a mission for the Lord in a very different place.

It was in that year that General Robert Johnston was offered the position of president of the Birmingham National Bank in Birmingham, Alabama. General Johnston's younger brother, Joseph, had called Alabama home for thirty years. He was already involved in banking and business interests in Birmingham and may have influenced this career opportunity for his brother. Joseph Johnston would be elected governor of Alabama six years later.

After being involved in many aspects of the Charlotte community for twenty years, it was hard for the Johnston family to pull up its roots and move to a rough and tumble mining and steel mill town. This would not be the genteel Charlotte to which Johnsie had become accustomed. She commented that her heart was so heavy upon leaving that she did not see "how the train could carry the extra load."[1]

Johnsie, however, tackled the move with the same indefatigable spirit that she had every other challenge in her life. In no time, the relocated family was involved in helping organize the South Highland Presbyterian Church. She also joined her first literary club, the Cadmean Circle, where she presented her first formal paper. A short time later, she founded the Highland Book Club and was appointed its first president, an office that she would hold for the next twenty-two years.[2]

The labor of love that would become Johnsie's life work was not something the devoted wife and mother had planned. While in Birmingham, her son Gordon was being tutored for his entrance into Princeton by a professor from Virginia. One day, Gordon asked permission to accompany his mentor to the Pratt Mines, where he was to lead a Bible study for the convicts who toiled there.* A few Sundays later, Johnsie made the trip with the professor and her son. Soon, General Johnston was also making the weekly trek.

Years later, Johnsie recalled the feeling that came over her upon entering the prison camp and seeing the boys and men enduring the oppressive conditions. Her thoughts went back to her father in the prison hospital and the promise she had made to help those in similar situations. That first Sunday at the mine was the first of ten years of Sundays in which Johnsie would lead a Bible study for the convicts. Through this experience, the Lord would continue to deal with Johnsie and clarify for her the exact nature of her calling. A fire had been kindled, but she needed to know where to focus the light.³

Some of that clarity came one Sunday afternoon when she witnessed a scene that would forever be a part of her. A boy sat on the front row with a simply dressed older woman who appeared to be his mother. A guard came and touched her on the arm indicating that it was time for her to leave. Immediately, the woman screamed and began clinging to the boy. The thought of leaving her son in such a place was more than she could bear.

"Oh, God is there no one to comfort my boy now?" she cried as the guard led her away.

Immediately, Johnsie responded to the plea with a prayer of her own. "If it be thy will, Lord," she whispered silently, "I will make some place for the little boys of Alabama, that they will be spared this place of wretchedness and contamination."⁴

Johnsie now had the inspiration and even began to talk openly of her dream. She simply did not know how and where to start. That important piece of the puzzle would fall into place one April afternoon. As she entered the prison, a hardened convict approached and asked for a few minutes of her time. Johnsie was surprised, for this was one of the prisoners that she never felt she had been able to reach.

---

*   During the latter part of the nineteenth century, Alabama and other states adopted the practice of leasing their convicts to private companies, such as railroads, mines, and timber interests. The convicts, including those underage, were actually housed at the worksites in crude, makeshift quarters. This became known as the "convict lease system."

"Oh, Mrs. Johnston, I am so glad to see you. I was afraid you might not come today," he said earnestly. "I want to help you on that boys' industrial school—the place you want to build to save boys from coming here. I don't want you to forget them."[5]

As he turned to walk away, he pressed an envelope into her hand. Busy with her duties that day at the mine, she put away the envelope and thought no more about it until she returned home that evening. Opening it, she found one hundred dollars—an amazing sum for most anyone in that day, but especially for an inmate serving a life term. Johnsie was touched by the man's sacrifice, but also by the Lord's blessing upon her task. That same prisoner would later add fifty more dollars to his donation. As promised, Johnsie saved the man's contribution for its intended purpose. She would always say that it was the most significant gift ever made to the Alabama Boys' Industrial School. To make her dream—and that of the lifer—a reality, a similar financial commitment would be required from many others.[6]

The convict's donation had effectively started the campaign. Now, Johnsie needed some allies for the larger battle that lay ahead. She found the first in the person of an old friend. Mrs. George Eager, the president of the Alabama Federation of Women's Clubs, asked Johnsie to attend the organization's first state convention in Selma. As an extension of some of her club activities, Johnsie was asked to prepare a literary paper entitled "Light, More Light" to those assembled. At the appointed time, she stepped behind the lectern and faced an assembly hall filled with women. She paused, turned to the moderator, and asked for permission to deviate from her stated address. She discarded her notes and began speaking from her heart about the atrocities many of the boys in Alabama were being subjected to through their imprisonment with hardened criminals. She shared real stories of boys being thrown in prison for stealing an empty jug or a pair of shoes. She told of boys whose lives were ruined by one simple mistake. She spoke of the need for a school where boys could be loved, shown discipline, and trained for a productive life.

At the conclusion, women came forward—many with tears in their eyes—to ask what could be done. Johnsie was ready with the answer: "You must go to the legislature of Alabama and ask for the establishment of an industrial school for boys." Just as her first speech to her father's overseer had turned the plow, this plea also broke new ground, as the Alabama Federation of Women's Clubs appointed a committee, with Johnsie as chair, to approach the legislature with just such a request.[7]

Johnsie decided that before she appealed to the legislature for funds, she needed some conception of what kind of boys' school she wanted. Her first visit would be to New York, and she was fortunate to have the perfect person to assist her in the form of Governor Theodore Roosevelt. Johnsie, of course, would say that fortune had nothing to do with it, that the Good Lord had put him in her path; and those who knew the lady's convictions would not dare to argue that point. Her son Gordon had served with Roosevelt's Rough Riders during the Spanish-American War and maintained a close relationship with the new governor.

Johnsie and Mrs. Eager were invited to meet with Roosevelt at the governor's mansion in Albany. They left with just what they wanted: a signed letter of introduction from the governor giving them entrée to any of New York's schools or institutions for boys. They visited, among others, the George Junior Republic in Freeville and the Berkshire Industrial Farm in Canaan and were especially impressed with the latter. On their trip home, they visited a school in Tennessee that particularly caught their attention. It was similar in concept to Berkshire, but depended heavily on private donations. This appealed to Johnsie, because she felt that anyone making a personal contribution to a cause would be more likely to maintain a long-term interest in its endeavors.[8]

With a clear vision in mind, Johnsie and her committee began lobbying the Alabama legislature. The women knew what they wanted their school to be and had prepared a written charter that provided for, among other features, a completely female board of directors. The most important weapon in their arsenal may have been one that would be almost impossible to defeat: a mother's love. In later years, Johnsie's niece described it well. "The women of Alabama had become mother-conscious under the sway of one woman's vision of a great love, and their motherhood had burst the walls of home and become state inclusive."[9]

The women of Alabama had formed an alliance based upon their shared love and compassion for the many nameless, faceless boys left to suffer among grown men in the state's penal system. Such collective emotion, when given its focus by someone as committed as Elizabeth "Johnsie" Johnston, was a powerful force.

Sensing that the women's cause had statewide support, the attorney general came out in support of the idea, and the legislature followed by passing a law creating the Alabama Boys' Industrial School. There was a catch, however, for the legislature failed to provide the requested $3,000; that funding would have to come separately from the Appropriations Committee. Discouraged but not deterred, Johnsie personally visited the attorney general at the suggestion of her brother-in-law, Governor Johnston. The meeting did not go well.

The attorney general essentially told Mrs. Johnston that she had a fine idea, but the men would take it from here. As a parting shot, he also inquired, "What in the world are you women doing meddling in our business? You better go home and mind your own children."

"What does your wife do with her time?" Johnsie shot back. "Does she ever play cards?"

"About six afternoons a week," he flippantly replied.

"Well, if we prefer teaching prisoners and looking after the welfare of the youth of your state to card playing, that's our business," she countered as she left the office.[10]

That salvo may have made Johnsie feel better, but it got them no closer to the Appropriations Committee. Nevertheless, the campaign continued. As the final days of the legislative session neared, one of the lawmakers came to see her with bleak advice.

"Mrs. Johnston, you might just as well go home. You can no more get your bill through the Legislature than you can move the Capitol."

"You go in and tell the men of Alabama that there is One behind this movement who can move mountains, the hills, and the whole world," she countered. "What is a little State Capitol to Him? We are going to save the little boys of Alabama, and if we can't get our bill before the Committee, I intend to stand in the rotunda of this Capitol all night and then give the story to every paper in the state. People are not scared of God, but they are of the papers!"[11]

Whether it was fear of the Almighty or the press, something she said must have gotten their attention. In a matter of moments, he was back with word that the Appropriations Committee would hear her. Put on the spot on a moment's notice, the situation got the best of the great lady. She felt it was one of her worst presentations ever, matched only by the apathy of her audience. She left the chamber feeling all hope was lost. As she stood in the rotunda, tired and discouraged, she felt the only chance of success was through the Lord's will.

As she stood lost in her thoughts, she was tapped on the shoulder by one of the committee members. "Mrs. Johnston, the committee has just passed favorably on your bill, but you will not have it, for it has been so much changed, it is not what you want," he stated. "My advice is for you to go home and come before the next legislature, and you will have better success."

"My boys can't wait," she replied. "Put it on the calendar like it is."

"Oh, you would not like it," he countered. "The changes are so vital; it is no longer the same bill."

"Put it on the calendar," she said flatly as she walked away.

She spent the night in Montgomery with emotions ranging from defeat to restlessness, anxiety to hope. As she walked to the train station the next morning planning to return to Birmingham, she passed a newspaper stand.

"Alabama Boys' Industrial Bill Passes Both Houses Last Night With An Appropriation of $3,000," read the headline. Below, she found the full text of the bill. Not a single word had been changed or omitted.

She immediately changed her plans and headed for the capitol. Upon arrival, she was greeted by many incredulous legislators asking how on earth she was able to get her bill passed. The answer could not be found on earth.

"It did not just happen, gentlemen," she affirmed. "It was God's work, and you men just could not stop it. That's all."[11]

3

A Mother's Love

Everyone has heard of that proverbial son that "only a mother could love." Well, the Alabama Boys' Industrial School had hundreds of them during its first fifty years. But, thankfully, it had not one, but seven mothers ready to provide the love and guidance these boys desperately needed.

That was just how Elizabeth Johnston envisioned her home for wayward boys. In the words of her niece years later, the founder wanted to bring "the mother love of home into the impersonal institution."[1] Beyond that, Mrs. Johnston also had strong beliefs about which of the sexes might be better equipped for such a challenge, and she shared them in one of her early reports to the governor. "Whatever may be the suspicion with which men may view the work of women, as a business matter, in caring for these boys, no man who has known a loving mother can fail to appreciate the fact that women know better how to deal with boys than men, and make money go farther than a man can. The Board would rejoice if they could feel that it was best to turn this whole work over to men chosen by the State, but they cannot be sure it would be best for the boys."[2]

With that in mind, the enacting legislation signed February 23, 1899, called for the new school to "be under the management and control of a board of directors which shall consist of seven ladies . . ."[3] Such a structure might not be so shocking in the twenty-first century, but it was unheard of in the United States at a time twenty years before women even had the right to vote. The Alabama Boys' Industrial School would become the first school of its kind with a board of directors comprised entirely of women.[4]

The first board was nominated by the governor and confirmed by the senate, and the members were to have staggered terms of office ranging from two to six years. After these initial terms of office, subsequent terms were to be for six years. "Thereafter," the charter stated, "the lady members of said board shall be elected by the continuing members thereof." In other words, the ladies of the board were given the right to choose their own members, and several of them served for many years thereafter.[5]

In addition to Mrs. Johnston, who served as the board's president, the initial members were Mrs. George B. Eager, Mrs. Erwin Craighead, Mrs. T. G. Bush, Mrs. E. S. Fitzpatrick, Mrs. S. D. Cole, and Mrs. James G. Converse. A few of these deserve special mention. Mrs. Eager, Mrs. Johnston's good friend from the Alabama Federation of Women's Clubs and also her traveling companion in touring some of the country's boys' schools, was elected vice-president. Mrs. Craighead, who was also active in the Federation of Women's Clubs, served on the board from 1899 until her death in 1926. She was an early advocate of vocational education, and the dining hall was eventually named in her honor. Mrs. Bush served as the treasurer of the board from 1899 until her death in 1930. It is said that she delighted in visiting the school to hear the band and view the military drills. Her con-

ABIS was the first institution of its kind to have an all-female board of directors. Mrs. Johnston (center) poses with two other board members in this undated photo.

suming interest, however, was in seeing "Christ's life emulated on campus." Mrs. Bush's dedication to her faith led her family to donate money for the campus chapel, which still stands as a tribute to her.[6]

The seven ladies had considerable power. They were authorized to select "employees as to them shall seem necessary or expedient, whose term of office or employment shall be for such time as the board may prescribe; and said board shall have the power to remove any such officer, agent or employee at any time, with or without cause." The charter further stipulated that "the board of directors have power to make such bylaws, rules and regulations, not inconsistent with the laws of this state, as shall be necessary or expedient for the government and management of said institution."[7]

So who were these sons of Alabama that were to be placed under the care, custody and control of these seven remarkable ladies? The state's first juvenile code, enacted in 1907, eight years after the ABIS was chartered, goes into considerable detail in describing this new legal designation known as the "juvenile delinquent."

> Be it enacted by the Legislature of Alabama, that any child under fourteen years of age, who violates any law of this State, or ordinance of any municipality thereof; or who is incorrigible; or who knowingly associates with thieves, gamblers, whores or vicious or immoral persons; or who is growing up in idleness or crime; or knowingly visits or enters a house of ill fame; or who knowingly visits or patronizes any policy shop, bucket shop, pool room, billiard room, bar room, or club room where liquors are sold; or where any gaming table, or device for gambling is or is operated, or who loiters about any such places; or who habitually smokes cigarettes; or who wanders about the streets at night without being on any lawful business; or who habitually wanders about any railroad yard or tracks; or jumps or hooks on to any moving engine or car; or unlawfully enters any engine or cab or habitually use vile, obscene, profane or indecent language; or is found in possession of any indecent or lascivious book, picture, pistol, dirk, bowie knife or knife of like kind or of brass knuckles; or is guilty of immoral conduct in any public place, or in or

about any school house; shall be deemed a juvenile delinquent person and shall be proceeded against, as such, in the manner hereinafter provided.[8]

The moral leaders of Alabama were obviously concerned about the evil influences that might have an impact on the state's youngsters. No further elaboration is required concerning thieves, gamblers and prostitutes, but policy shops and bucket shops are not part of today's vernacular. A policy shop was an establishment where men wagered on commodity prices. In a time before betting on sports, gambling on the price of cotton or hogs had to do. A bucket shop was a place that sold beer by the bucket.

Who could imagine a time when "jumping onto a moving engine or car" was such a problem that it deserved special mention in the juvenile code? It was more common than most imagine, as will be seen elsewhere in this book. As far as some of the other offenses mentioned, it is staggering to conceive the numbers of teenagers who would be lined up outside today's juvenile courts if children were still routinely hauled in for "wandering about the streets at night without being on any lawful business," using "profane or indecent language," or possessing an "indecent or lascivious book."

The new juvenile code applied to youngsters of both races but did not address the uneven situation in the correction of delinquents. While white youth would be sent to ABIS, black youth would continue to be confined in county and state facilities with adults until 1911 when the Alabama Industrial School for Negro Children was established in Mt. Meigs.

Nevertheless, the above was the working definition of a juvenile delinquent, and the new school on the eastern side of Birmingham had a place for those who were not black. The school's charter described the type of youngster that could be admitted to the school, specifically, white males "between the ages of six and eighteen who, by their cause of conduct or surrounding, are likely to become base or criminal or hurtful to the state, or the best interests of society, to be committed to the keeping of said school under the provisions of this act . . ."[9] The document went on to provide examples such as begging, being abandoned, not attending school, idling away one's time on the streets, being orphans or paupers, having parents who were drunkards or imprisoned, and last and presumably not least, having been arrested and brought before the police courts of the state.[10]

Undoubtedly in an effort to prevent more occurrences like Mrs. Johnston had witnessed at the mines, the institution's charter specifically addressed matters of a more serious nature that heretofore had caused young men to be sentenced to the penitentiary.

"Be it further enacted," it decreed, "that when any white child between the ages of six and sixteen years shall have been tried and convicted of any crime, punishable by imprisonment, in the penitentiary or in jail or by hard labor for the county, before any court of this State, the Court may, if of opinion that the interests of the child would thereby be promoted, sentence such child to commitment to said school, in lieu of such imprisonment or hard labor for the county."[11]

Those empowered to commit boys to the school were any justice of the supreme court, chancellor, judge of probate, circuit judge, or judge of any city or criminal court of Alabama. In a marked departure from how the juvenile justice system of today operates, the charter also allowed a parent or guardian to commit his or her child, or for a boy to commit himself voluntarily to the institution.[12]

If one reads the 1907 juvenile code and the ABIS charter carefully, it is easy to see that there was considerable inconsistency surrounding the handling of juvenile matters. In some cases, it is stated that a juvenile must be under the age of fourteen, in other cases the dividing age is sixteen, and in some situations a youth could be sent to ABIS if he was simply under eighteen. In most every instance, a boy could be kept in custody until his twenty-first birthday. Cases involving underage offenders were also being heard by a variety of different courts subject to the whims and legal interpretations of a countless number of judges. Most of this confusion was finally clarified by 1915 when amendments made to the Alabama Juvenile Code established the juvenile age as under sixteen, where it remained until the 1970s.

So, the new Alabama Boys' Industrial School had quite an assortment of young men ranging in age from six to twenty-one for offenses running the gamut from a smoking cigarette to a smoking gun. The success of the school would not only require an ample portion of motherly love, but also all of the talent and energy these seven women could muster.

4

Building on Faith

A person of lesser faith would suggest that an unusual set of events *conspired* to make the Alabama Boys' Industrial School a reality. On the contrary, Elizabeth Johnston insisted that her heavenly father *inspired* an unlikely collection of individuals to accomplish that feat.

When asked about the success of the school, Mrs. Johnston had no doubt about her answer. "We do not reply upon money or equipment," she replied. "We ask God to guide and direct us. We have tried in every way to honor Him, and in return He has wrought miracles in our behalf."[1]

The first of these miracles involved the very acquisition of the land where the campus would eventually take shape. One day soon after the passage of the bill authorizing the school, Mrs. Johnston was riding in a buggy with a real estate salesman just east of Birmingham. The pair happened upon an elderly man who was hitchhiking on the road and stopped to give him a ride. As they rode, Mrs. Johnston told the old man, known as Uncle Van to those in the area, about her plans for a boys' school and the reason for their afternoon excursion.

Mrs. Johnston was describing the type of land she envisioned when Uncle Van suddenly called for the salesman to stop. "Right here is the very spot you are looking for, lady," he declared. The three climbed out of the buggy and began surveying the scene before them. "It's perfect," Mrs. Johnston concluded, "like forever living in the Twenty-third Psalm."[2]

In a subsequent report to the governor, she elaborated further on the 136-acre site. "The situation is naturally most beautiful, with lovely views of the mountains and valleys, while three bold springs of pure water arise in the center of it and afford excellent facilities, not only for the supply of water necessary for the premises, but for purposes of irrigation also. The

The log cabin in the foreground, as well as the barn, were the only existing structures on the property chosen for the school. The cabin served as the school's home until other buildings could be erected.

land has a good clay subsoil; is level or slightly rolling, and can be brought to a high state of cultivation and fertility."[3]

With a donation of $3,000 from the Commercial Club of Birmingham, the board purchased the property, probably in 1899, and began preparations for its occupancy. The existing structures were an old barn and a dilapidated two-room log cabin. The first boys lived in the log cabin until their numbers reached a point that a tent had to be erected for the overflow. The board authorized the construction of a three-story wooden building to provide dormitory space, industrial shops, and classrooms. The cost of this project came almost entirely from donated money, material, and labor obtained by Mrs. Johnston.[4]

How she acquired these gifts is another example of the extraordinary events that came together in the founding of the school. Her search for lumber is a case in point. One day she decided to go to a lumberyard in Saginaw, between Birmingham and Montgomery. At the train station, she asked the dispatcher if the express train could stop to let her off at Saginaw.

"The express stop at Saginaw?" he laughed. "Why, that's impossible. Why do you want me to do this unheard of thing?"

She sweetly told him of her boys and the need for better accommodations and the lumber to build those quarters. The gentleman slowly shook his head and called to someone in the adjoining room, "Have the No. 4 express slow up at Saginaw for Mrs. R. D. Johnston."[5]

When she reached the lumberyard in Saginaw the next day, more surprises awaited. She approached the owner, Mr. Morris, prepared to make her plea, but was interrupted before she could even begin. Morris slammed his fist down on the table and said forcefully, "You have come for lumber

Mrs. Johnston in a photo from one the school's early annual reports.

for that boys' school and I want to tell you that it's the grandest thing ever started in the state of Alabama. Just tell me what you want me to give and you shall have it."[6]

As Mrs. Johnston stood speechless, he took her list and began poring over it. Finally he told her that he could provide part of the lumber, but that his mill did not cut some of the heavier timber that she needed. "You go over to the Marbury lumberyard and tell them I said give you that." She hurried back to the station to catch the train for Montgomery. Upon reaching Marbury's lumberyard, she told of Mr. Morris's gift and asked the manager if he could supply the remainder. He marked off a quantity of lumber he would furnish and handed her back the list with these further directions, "Now go down to Wadsworth's yard, about ten miles out, and tell him I said to give you the rest."

At the end of the day, she rode back to Birmingham in the caboose of a forty-car freight train filled with more than $1,500 (approximately $41,666 in 2014 dollars) of lumber donated by the three lumberyards.[7]

On many occasions when lumber and other materials arrived at the station in Birmingham, Mrs. Johnston would hail horse-drawn wagons and ask the driver to carry the cargo out to the school at no charge. She used the same strategy to enlist carpenters, brick masons, and other workers to donate their time. Most of the time, after hearing Mrs. Johnston's story, the men agreed, sensing they were doing something worthwhile.[8]

Toward the end of 1900, with the first building almost complete, some additional materials were still needed. Mrs. Johnston went to another lumberyard and asked if she could have some material on credit until she could afford to pay. She received a flat refusal. Undaunted, she left knowing that her Lord would provide a way just like he had every time previously. Two days later, the man called and said that she could have whatever she needed and pay for it when she could. She asked what had changed his mind.

"Well, Mrs. Johnston," he replied, somewhat bewildered, "I just have to do this because of a dream I had . . ." Mrs. Johnston stopped him in mid-sentence; no further explanation was needed.[9]

Mrs. Johnston just knew that the second building, begun in 1903, was going to be easier. The State of Alabama had appropriated $3,000 for its construction and all appeared well. When the money was due, however, the state reneged on its pledge, citing more pressing financial needs. For the first time since her efforts began, she felt defeated and even feared bankruptcy. Some of her supporters suggested she seek a loan, but she believed the prospects of that unlikely since they had little collateral upon which to base their request.

As usual, the devout lady prayed for guidance. "Lord, show me the way. I am lost, and if You expect me to do this work, You will have to direct my path."

A few days later, she found herself in town, searching for an answer, looking for a sign. As she walked down the street, she looked up and saw the words Steiner Brothers Bank. She went in, asked to see the president, and was ushered into the office of Mr. Burghard Steiner. She told him her story of the boys' home, of the great need, and of the state's failure to live up to its obligations.

After a moment, the large, courteous man with the thick beard replied, "A bank is in business to make money and cannot make a loan without security for repayment. The bank cannot lend you the money." As Mrs. Johnston's heart sank, he continued, "But I will let you have it personally. How much do you need?"

Mr. Steiner wrote her his personal check. She thanked him warmly for his generosity and moved toward the door, but Mr. Steiner had one last question. "Why did you come to me?" he asked.

"I called upon the Lord in distress," she quoted from the 118th Psalm. "The Lord answered me, and set me in a large place." The money was repaid on time, although Mr. Steiner refused to accept any interest. He became a lifelong friend and supporter of the school.[10]

Mrs. Johnston learned to trust the Lord not only in a major crisis, but in the smaller day-to-day problems as well. As boys began moving into the new buildings, the demand often exceeded the available space. During one such period, she heard that five little boys were bound for the penitentiary unless someone intervened. She told the superintendent to make room for them.

"But," he replied, "we have no beds."

"Well, make pallets," she said.

"But, there are no mattresses," he tried to explain.

"Take the boys, and I'll get the mattresses," she ended the discussion.

As this woman of faith left the office in pursuit of those mattresses, she was called back to the telephone. "Mrs. Johnston," a voice said, "I wonder if you could use a dozen mattresses at the school?"

"I should say I could," was her answer. After experiencing so many similar miracles, she was no longer even surprised.[11]

5

The Start Is Made

The three boys toed the line that had been scratched in the dirt and then raced toward the entrance on C. D. Griffin's count of three. As the two older boys scaled the wooden gate, the youngest—Jimmie—crawled through an opening in the fence, thus earning the honor of being the first student of the Alabama Boys' Industrial School.[1]

C. D. Griffin was the first superintendent of the Alabama Boys' Industrial School, being hired by the board in April of 1900 for an annual salary of $600, and presumably his room and board. Little is known about his background other than the fact that he resigned a similar position in another state to accept the task.[2]

Griffin's experiences in providing the care, supervision, and training for these three boys and the others to follow during his first fifteen months on the job are found in his meticulously detailed handwritten diary covering both the important and the innocuous aspects of life at the school. He touched on the chores and daily activities that engaged the staff and the boys, as well as many of the expenditures he made to keep the institution running. Most revealing were the stories of the boys, with the challenges and rewards of supervising these sons of mischief.[3]

Griffin's initial entry on Friday, June 22, 1900, gave an account of how the first three boys came to be students at the school.

"Went to meet Mrs. Cole and Mrs. Johnston to see about some boys. We found three boys, Jim _____, 10 years old, who has a poor home. He was willing to come to the school, and Slawson _____, 13, had not been at home for several weeks, but was willing to come to the school, Rufus _____, 12, whose mother sent a note giving her consent for the boy to come to the school. The boys were dirty, ragged, and showed neglect, but were bright. We invested in some bedding

and provisions and started for East Lake. The Chief of Police told me we had three of the very worst boys in town."

Much of the early travel to and from the school on the outskirts of Birmingham was made by streetcars, and such was the case as Griffin escorted this impish trio who looked like anything but the "worst boys in town." Accompanied by two men who would be working with Griffin at the school, they made their way to their new home.

"*The boys attracted much attention on the cars. John and Evans were attending a funeral, so we had to wait for them, so it was quite late before we left East Lake. The boys were given their supper and put to bed. The start is made. I brought home 25 cents' worth of bread and paid for it.*"

Over the next few days, Griffin got a good dose of what life would be like on the farm, confronting one little crisis after another. To begin with, such heavy rain greeted the new family on their first night that Griffin commented, *"everything was afloat in the morning."* The road leading into

This photograph from an early souvenir booklet shows the boys gathered in the dining room of the old log cabin. These are most likely the first students in the school. One of the men in the background is Superintendent C. D. Griffin, and the other is his assistant John Embree.

the property was *"filled with water nearly to the buggy box."* That day, Griffin made another trip into town, where he arranged to buy groceries wholesale, and purchased fifty pounds of flour, a case of syrup, fifty pounds of meal, a ham, some sidemeat, fifty pounds of sugar, and fifty cents' worth of bread. Upon return he *"found the boys had done fairly well. Had picked a pail of blackberries."*

That first Sunday proved to be anything but a day of rest. On the contrary, *"four lengths of fence were down and cattle were everywhere,"* Griffin wrote. *"John took the boys, drove the cattle out and fixed the fence."* Later in the day, there were other intruders besides cows. *"After dinner, we had visitation from a lot of boys from town, but as visitors are not allowed on the place on Sunday, I soon drove them off."*

In the evening, Griffin had his first bit of trouble with the boys in his charge, probably precipitated by the unwanted guests earlier in the day.

"Our three boys were rather homesick to see their friends and began to cry. Having had no chance to bathe them Saturday, I wanted to have them bathe and change clothes. Jimmie's pants were so torn that he was about naked. I had nothing to put on him but a pair of overalls, but he "didn't want to put on them overalls." *Before the boys would settle down and mind, I had to spank Jimmie. That straightened them all out and I succeeded in getting them bathed and clean new shirts on them. We went for a walk and when we returned to the house I read to them and the day ended very serenely."*

Much of the work those first few months revolved around preparing the land and constructing the first building. Griffin noted that first week the boys *"fixed the gate and the roadway by the gate"* and also *"worked on the underbrush where we want to put a bridge for our driveway,"* while another entry stated that the *"carpenters worked on the building until they ran out of lumber."* While workers toiled on the building, the boys were involved in more routine activities. *"John and the boys prepared the ground and set out the tomato plants. The new hoes helped prepare the ground much better than the old."*

Just as would be required of such an operation today, there was always a little public relations to be done. In an entry from June 28, Griffin wrote, *"Mrs. Johnston invited a number of ladies who were attending the Teacher's Institute in Birmingham to come see the school. The ladies were all over the house* and were much amused at our kitchen and dining room in the old log house. One of the visitors was a writer preparing an article on the school."

On June 29, Griffin mentioned a new arrival. *"I received a telephone from Mrs. Johnston that a boy at Mercy Home was a fit subject for our school. I communicated with Mrs. Ramsey at the house and found the particulars about the boy. The father is a drunkard and is very abusive to the boy. The mother was with him at the house and did not dare take the boy back home as the father was very brutal. The boy too large for the house. I told Mrs. Ramsey to have the mother meet me at the Exchange and I would take the boy with me. The mother met me there with her boy and he came home with me."*

As July began, Griffin had to contend with the first of what would be a continuing series of problems with his staff. On July 2 he wrote, *"Our cook, George Murray, left us. We are not as well equipped as he would like so our plebian way of living does not suit his fastidious taste. He left us for town and I am once more 'chief cook.'"* The next day brought another resignation. *"Our teamster, Parker, came to tell us that he could work for us no longer. He wanted a check for the balance due him, but I sent him to General Johnston to settle as the contract had been made with him. Having no one to drive the mules, John and the boys utilized them by plowing in the garden, preparing more ground for a crop."* But, at least, things were going well with one of the hired hands. *"Our wash woman came to do the washing and ironing. She did very nicely. Was through about three o'clock. Charged us 65 cents."*

Also on July 3rd, Griffin decided to put Jimmie, the recipient of the previous week's spanking, to a little test. *"I thought of an experiment to see how far Jimmie could be trusted. I sent him on an errand to Mrs. Cole's at Woodlawn. Gave him a note to Mr. Smithson so Mr. Smithson would take care of the horse. Gave a note with check enclosed to car conductor and note for Mrs. Cole. Jimmie reached home safely on Dollie about one o'clock with a note from Mrs. Cole and a package of boys' clothing which will be very acceptable. Mrs. Cole had given the boy a lunch, so he did not need any dinner. I am much pleased with my experiment and Mrs. Cole was much pleased also."*

The next day, Independence Day, brought a myriad of activities and a slight setback with Jimmie. *"It does not seem much like Independence Day. Could hear no noise of firecrackers all of the forenoon. I tried to get some firecrackers* when in town Monday, but could find none on sale, but there would be plenty of them the next day so they told me. I wanted to get some for our boys to fire off. The boys played all of the forenoon. We had an extra good dinner. After we had the work done, I dressed the boys in some clothing that had been donated to us. Just as I was going to dress Jimmie, his mother and a man companion appeared on the scene. Of course, the dressing had to be postponed, but Jimmie came and wanted to go just as the boys were starting. I told him I wouldn't have time to dress him now, so he would have to stay home. The mother was very angry and said Jimmie had no business to come out here in the first place, and said she was going to have the boy out of here at once, as he had a good home to go to, etc., etc. I told her while the boy was here he would have to mind. She stayed about an hour and visited with the boy."

The remainder of July was fairly mundane. Work continued on the new building, with gravel, sand, and building materials being delivered on a regular basis. Plastering and flooring was done in the building, and the boys and staff began moving in on July 18. Griffin seemed quite pleased by this development, as he wrote, *"Put up a bed in the bedroom and used the rooms. Seems very nice to sleep in a bed again. We are getting very comfortably settled."*

Toward the end of the month several incidents occurred that were somewhat outside the norm. On Sunday, July 22, Griffin remarked, *"Not long after dinner, a caller came. It proved to be Mr. _____ from Montgomery with his son Jacob, 12 years old, whom he wanted to enter the school. Mr. Huff brought a letter of recommendation from Mrs. Eager. The boy would not stay at home nights and consequently the father could not control him and brought him here. Our first boy from out of town. He seems a very quiet, pleasant child."*

The next day, there was an accident quite typical of a bunch of boys that involved who else but Jimmie. *"Tonight while milling, the boys were playing with the stock. Jimmie had been riding Romeo. He was off and trying to jump on again. Romeo stood by a large rock. Jimmie jumped too hard and slid clear over, falling on the rock and cutting quite a gash in his head. He cried; his wound bled profusely. We got him to the house, washed off the blood, and put on some sticking plaster. He was alright in a little while."*

In the early 1900s, those of Italian descent often endured discrimination in the South similar to that of African Americans. While not overt,

Griffin's diary nevertheless revealed a hint of prejudice between the lines in a July 23rd entry. *"A man called today with a woman and two boys. Italians. The man spoke quite well but the woman did not seem to understand 'United States.' The man explained that the woman was his cousin and she wanted to put her two boys with the school. The Chief of Police was to send them out and the brothers wanted to see the place first. I took the necessary statistics and they said the boys would be out tomorrow."*

A note the next day closed this episode by stating simply, *"Our Italian boys did not put in an appearance."* They are not mentioned again.

A paragraph from July 26th is illustrative of the unusual offenses that might lead to a boy being referred to the school. *"Mr. and Mrs. _____ of East Lake called to see about putting a son here. He is 15 years old and will not stay at home. Has been off with a circus for several months. He was away from home when they came here. Had been gone for several days. They seem to be very nice people and greatly worried about their son. Mr. and Mrs. _____ said they would bring their boy right here as soon as he came home."*

Two days later, the wayfaring circus traveler returned. *"The new boy John, whose father and mother, the _____, came to see me a few days ago, was here and seemed to be enjoying himself with the other boys. I think John a pretty good sort of a boy and hope we can help him."*

Sunday, August 5th, proved significant in the life of the new institution. *"I met Mrs. Johnston and her baby at ten o'clock. I had dressed the boys in their Sunday clothes, so they made quite a presentable appearance. I was very thankful that we had the piano so we could use it. We had some singing and then Mrs. Johnston had a Sunday School class. The first Sunday services in connection with the Alabama Industrial School. Ten boys, as follows: Raymond, Pat and Fred (brothers), Jimmie, Slawson, Henry, Rufus, John, Charlie and Jacob. Dinner passed off very nicely and then Mrs. Johnston had a quick talk with the boys. I took Mrs. Johnston and baby back to the station about four o'clock. We had a very nice sing after supper. The boys sing well and seem to enjoy it."*

The next day, a figure almost as well-known to the boys as Mrs. Johnston made an appearance at the school. *"Judge Feagin and Mr. Meade, Clerk of the Court, came to make the institution a visit. They watched the boys work and made a complete examination of the building and made many inquiries in regard to our needs, aims, etc. Our company seemed to enjoy supper in our primitive dining room. The boys behaved very nicely and were much complimented by our guests."*

Tuesday marked three straight days of relative tranquility, as described by Griffin. *"Had supper early and the boys had a good time playing after supper. It was a beautiful evening. They had a great time playing sheepfold in the moonlight."* According to most accounts, sheepfold was a popular game in which a group of children would join hands in a large circle while one child would chase another who was trying to break through into the safety of the sheepfold.

As the institution neared two months of operation, another group of boys on the way were much more interested in leaving the sheepfold than entering, and they made the previous antics of Jimmie seem like child's play.

6

SPURGEON AND OTHER HEADACHES

The relatively peaceful days of the first two months became fewer and fewer as the dog days of August descended upon the growing school. As the age, size, and behavioral problems of the new enrollees increased, so did C. D. Griffin's headaches. No student embodied these frustrations more than a teenager named Spurgeon.

Griffin's introduction to Spurgeon should have provided a clue, as noted in his diary on August 21st. *"Miss _____ called with a note from Mrs. Johnston asking me to take her brother if possible. As Miss _____ thought he would be a hard boy to control and hard to keep here, we decided it would be best to wait till we had the lock on the dormitory door before we attempted to care for him. At present we have 11 boys and the dormitory door wide open."*

On another subject, the day did provide something positive as it may have planted a seed that would later germinate into something very fruitful for the school. *"At five o'clock I dressed the boys all up. We boarded the lumber wagon and went to the National Guard Encampment down near East Lake. The boys behaved very nicely. The band playing and drilling interested them very much indeed."*

A week later, some of the rebellious behavior that would plague Griffin for months began in earnest. After spending the day in Birmingham running errands, Griffin returned home to find trouble. *"When I reached home found Charlie _____ had succeeded in getting away from Mrs. Prey. I took Jimmie in a buggy and went in search. Met John with the wagon the other side of East Lake. They had caught the runaway boy. I had obtained a pair of shackles from Judge Feagin for use on runaway boys. Sloss and Charlie are still wearing chains. Fastened the shackles on the ankles of Sloss and Charlie."*

The diary did not state what indiscretion Sloss had committed, but it landed him in the same predicament as Charlie. Two days later, Griffin wrote: *"At five o'clock we loaded all but Sloss and Charlie into the wagon and took them to see the soldiers drill. Sloss and Charlie are still wearing chains and are somewhat mortified."*

Griffin was somewhat offended himself the following Saturday after a conversation with General Johnston, his boss's husband. Griffin had gone into Birmingham to report on the damage caused by a night of torrential rain, and his assessment was not well received. *"The General thought I was mistaken about the water, wanted to know why I had not plowed and sowed a patch of turnips, said I had all the time there was, said for me to come home, and have the manure hauled out. They do not seem to realize that we are living with no conveniences but are doing the best we can with what we have. I was so completely discouraged by the General's questioning that I came home at once and will say no more if the rain undermines the house."*

Things got no better for Griffin over the following days. John, his right-hand man, fell and twisted an ankle, resulting in several days' bed rest; the wash woman quit and a replacement had to be found; and another of the boys, John, ran away only to be brought back in shackles. To top it off, he received a visit from his favorite general. *"General and Mrs. Johnston and two daughters showed up at a very inconvenient time for visit. Very busy and because Mrs. Johnston was not familiar with road, I had to drive to the further corner of our land to take them back very late. After returning from seeing them to the main road, I had my supper to eat, boys to put to bed, milking to do, etc. It was quite late when I finally had my work done."*

His work was about to get harder, for on September 24th, the long-awaited Spurgeon arrived on campus. *"A short time after breakfast, two men came, one a sheriff or policeman, and with them was Spurgeon _____ and his belongings. Spurgeon is a very large boy and there had been quite a scene at the home where the boy was arrested as he declared he would 'get even' with the mother and sisters for having him sent here. He is a pretty hard case. Very large for his age—16 years—and very revengeful.*

Only three days later, Spurgeon made his presence known. *"Miss _____ called early in the forenoon and paid $8.50 for Spurgeon's care for a month. Spurgeon was very dramatic and would not speak to his sister. He made such*

A group of the school's earliest students are shown in this picture taken by fellow student James Dawsey in the early 1900s. It is not difficult to detect a little mischief in their faces.

a fool of himself I finally took him downstairs. Miss _____ felt very bad about her reception but was not at all astonished."

The next day, Griffin reported that *"Spurgeon ran away. John Embree jumped on Dollie and gave chase. I helped later, but we both returned without him. Went to town and purchased candy for boys. Found Spurgeon being detained at home in shackles and seemed subdued. We hope to send him to Nashville very soon."*

The next day, Griffin provided this update on their problem child. *"Spurgeon still wears shackles. For nearly a week now, I have slept in the dormitory near Spurgeon so as to be prepared if there should be any outbreak."*

Whether it was an act of hopelessness or hopefulness, Griffin was soon ready to give Spurgeon a try at home according to this entry dated October 17th.

"Miss L. came to see Spurgeon. I recommended his going out on parole if he would promise to behave. Miss L. has a job promised him. Spurgeon seemed much pleased at the prospect of going home and very willingly signed a paper that he would obey his mother in all things, keep away from bad company and theatres. He is to go sometime next week if he behaves himself. I file his promises with this paper. John took his shackles off this evening after supper and the boy seems perfectly happy."

Spurgeon was not the only boy giving Griffin fits—literally. *"Before we were ready to leave the table this morning, Ernest _____, our new boy, showed signs of having a fit. I had John take him downstairs and he had quite a violent time. I wrote a note to Mrs. Johnston asking what to do with him as we had no time to look after him. I sent the note by Jimmie. Mrs. Johnston said for me to take him to town and have him sent to the poor farm."*

Even with all the excitement involving Spurgeon and company, life carried on at the school. An example of the day-to-day minutia included a trip to Red Mountain to gather nuts, the usual Sunday evening sing-alongs, frequent visits from Mrs. Johnston and her friends, and of course, the weekly baths, as described by the superintendent in his entry for Sunday, November 11th.

"A very busy day. Water too cold for the boys to use the creek and house full of company Saturday and were too busy for the boys to bathe last week at all, so it must be done today. After breakfast had two boilers of water put on the

cook stove in the playroom and our three tubs put in the room. Boys had to bring water from the spring and carry the water out after bathing. Of course it took a long time to bathe 15 boys in this way, so it was nearly noon when I was through and could turn the boys over to John and change my own clothes."

On November 27th, the school celebrated its first Thanksgiving. A Mrs. Walter in Woodlawn donated a full dinner for the boys, and Mr. Prey and John _____ went in the wagon to pick it up. The lone sour note of the day came when a boy named Chester tried to pull a ruse in the presence of his parents. Griffin explained it like this:

"During the forenoon, Mr. and Mrs. _____ called to see their son. He had a very pitiful tale to tell. He had left off his underwear so as to tell his mother I wouldn't let him wear it. He told the boys he was going to leave off his shoes and stockings so to tell them the same story. His mother felt for a while that her darling boy was dreadfully abused, but when the other boys informed her that he left his underwear off without my knowing it, she said Chester was a really good boy only that he would not mind, would lie, and would not stay at home evenings. The father seemed to think that the boy was in the proper place and said that he should stay here till his record was what it should be."

There was one positive development for the day. "According to an agreement made some time ago with Johnnie _____ and his parents, I let Johnnie go home on parole today. I think he will be alright and he promises to sign a paper tomorrow to that effect."

On December 5th, Ernest _____, the fitful one, made his return. "During my absence, Mrs. _____ came with her son and a letter from Judge Feagin saying he was anxious to come back. Mrs. _____ brought some medicine for the boy to take four times a day, some pills to take occasionally, and a bottle marked 'poison' and a syringe. When he has a fit, he is to be given two drops of the 'poison' liquid, in a severe case four, but never more than five under any circumstances. Had I been at home I should have refused to accept him. As it was, I told him I would keep him until he had one of his spells and then he must go back to town as we could not afford to spend the time to watch him as there were so few of us. We are sorry for the boy as he appears to be a nice little fellow, but his mother wants to shirk the responsibility of caring for him."

Over a period of three days in early January, two new boys were sent to the school for most unusual offenses by today's standards. One boy, Edgar, age fourteen, was sentenced for stealing rides on trains. Hovater, age seventeen, took it a step further by beating his way onto trains.

A much more serious offense is mentioned on January 27th. *"While we were eating breakfast a ring at the front doorbell was followed by the ushering in of Mr. Powers of Mobile, son of the Sheriff there, and a boy, John _____, sentenced to us for manslaughter for five years. It seems his mother lives on the street leading to the canning factory and the factory girls have been in the habit of throwing stones at the house when passing to and from the factory. It was very annoying and one night the girls were extra boisterous and the owner of the house tried to catch them and called to John to bring his pistol. He had a very small pocket pistol. He ran into the house, brought it and fired, killing one of the girls instantly. His mother was sentenced to the pen as accessory to the murder."*

For whatever reason, parole must not have worked out for Spurgeon, for he reappeared in this entry from January 30th concerning a benefit program the boys were attending. *"Spurgeon always blunders so in drilling and makes such a fool of himself when there are any ladies around that we thought best not to take him. The new boy John from Mobile has not learned to drill and I had no 'Sunday clothes' for him and Hovater, our convict boy, is wearing chains yet, so I did not think best to take him. We left these three boys with Mr. Melton. Boys very well behaved. Boys remarked that they had never had a better time in their lives."*

On February 1st, another new resident, Clarence, was brought to the school and made quite an impression on Griffin. *"He was so dirty and filthy that I wanted to handle him with tongs. Did not look as though he had ever bathed and did not seem to know how to bathe. I put his clothing on the stove and burned it up."* His stay, however, was short-lived, for on February 12th, Griffin conceded that *"The Board decided we could not keep Clarence as he is so near an imbecile we could not bother with him and it was thought best to send him back to the mines."* In that day "imbecile" was regularly used in referring to a mentally deficient person.

On March 25th, the school narrowly averted a disaster. *"The clouds became so dark we could not see to do anything. The wind was very high and drove the water through the roof and under the doors till there was not a room in the house without water all over everything. We were more fortunate, however, than people in Birmingham for they had a regular cyclone there. Fourteen people killed and a large number wounded."*

A few days later, a storm of another type was brewing on campus. *"The boys reported that Spurgeon had asked the boys to run away with him if Mr. Embree went to town. He has been trying for some time to stir up the boys to run away. And when a plot of his to get about six of the boys to run away with him was unearthed, I promised the next one who mentioned the subject of running away some punishment. So, stopped long enough to put Spurgeon in the dungeon. Then went on to town. In the evening, we old folks colored about 90 Easter eggs for the boys after the boys had gone to bed."*

The next day, as the boys attended church services and celebrated with Easter eggs and candy, Spurgeon remained in the dungeon.

The diary did not divulge when Spurgeon again saw the light of day, but the ever-conniving youngster was at it again on May 27th. *"Spurgeon had taken advantage of my absence and had run away again. He was plowing in the onion patch and when at the other end of the patch from Felix, he deliberately left his mule and ran."* A week later, the fearless fugitive was captured and returned to the dungeon.

By July 5th, Spurgeon had earned his release from the dungeon and was back on the farm under the care of Felix. Using the same modus operandi as before, the determined delinquent once again left his mule and plow in the dust. In the diary's last mention of Spurgeon on July 15th, the superintendent paid Mr. McDaniel, the local constable, five dollars for his capture.

About two weeks later, according to the diary, the school celebrated the first anniversary of the laying of the cornerstone on the main building. As the school family assembled around the cornerstone, chances are Spurgeon had a front-row seat from the dungeon below.[1]

Griffin's diary comes to a mysterious end on September 12, 1901. It is not known whether the remainder has been lost or for some reason Griffin simply stopped keeping his daily account of the school's happenings. What is known is that Griffin submitted his resignation in June 1904 and the board accepted. There were references in the next year's annual report to "dissatisfaction among the employees,"[2] and in a subsequent report Mrs.

Johnston alluded to "debts incurred without our knowledge by the first superintendent."³ Dr. Hall, the minister who recruited Griffin's successor, simply said that the superintendent's "ideas were not in accord with those of the Board."⁴

Upon Griffin's resignation, the board acquired the services of William Connelley, an executive on loan from the local Tennessee Coal and Iron Company to serve as interim superintendent. Although Connelley served only a year while a permanent superintendent was found, he created the beginnings of a foundation on which the center of rehabilitation flourished, most notably with the "Open Door System" that Weakley also incorporated to create a caring atmosphere.

Perhaps it is the gracious David Weakley, who became superintendent in 1905, who summed up Griffin's resignation best when he wrote, "I never knew Mr. Griffin, so I am in no position to comment on his successes, nor his failures. No doubt, due to lack of money, divided public opinion, and often public hostility, he suffered many heartbreaks and disappointments."⁵

7

WE HAD TO GO

David Weakley thought he was where he was supposed to be in October 1904. He was on the staff at the Tennessee Industrial School, and he and his wife were happy in their work. But God, and one of his most persistent children, Elizabeth Johnston, thought otherwise.

Weakley was born on June 12, 1878, in Newbern, Tennessee, the son of a Confederate soldier. His family had been prominent and Weakley County was named for his ancestors. He received his education in the local public schools, followed by studies at Newbern Seminary. He had also completed special courses in vocational education, business administration, psychology, and mental hygiene.

In 1898, Weakley went to work as the manual training instructor at the Tennessee Industrial School in Nashville. This school, one of the first of its kind in the South, had been founded in 1885 by Edmund W. Cole after he was touched by the large number of children orphaned by the recent cholera epidemic in the city. Professor William Kilvington became the school's first superintendent and subsequently the mentor of David Weakley.[1]

"Professor Kilvington was a man of rare ability, charm, and attainments," Weakley said years later, "and whatever success I may have had, I owe mainly to his teaching and training, and I know of no one during my time who has made a more lasting contribution to the welfare of the children of the nation."[2]

In 1902, Weakley married Katherine Stamps, a recent graduate of Peabody College, who had been hired to teach at the industrial school. With Weakley's promotion to assistant superintendent of the school in 1903, the young couple appeared to have their future mapped out in Nashville.[3]

It was in the next autumn that Johnsie and the board members dispatched Dr. J. D. Hall, a Birmingham Episcopal minister, to visit Weakley. Hall informed the twenty-six-year-old schoolmaster that the board had been studying such institutions as his around the nation and was impressed with the educational and vocational programs, as well as the overall atmosphere, that his Tennessee school offered. Hall also told Weakley about Mrs. Johnston and the fledgling school in Alabama. The minister informed the young administrator about Mrs. Johnston's experiences teaching in the mines and her vision for the state's boys. He related her efforts in convincing both the populace and the legislature of the critical need for such a school, and the passage of the bill creating the school with its all-female board of directors.

Finally, Hall got around to sharing that the board was dissatisfied with the current superintendent, and asked Weakley if he might be interested in the position.

Years later, Weakley recalled that he was initially reluctant. He thought that the women were probably a "bunch of daydreamers, fault-finders, and busy-bodies" who would be difficult to work with on a daily basis, and he tactfully admitted as much to his visitor. Hall quickly told him otherwise and praised the board members as "level-headed, Christian persons whose only interest was to do something really worthwhile to advance the welfare of their less fortunate little brothers; that they were giving their time, money and themselves to a most worthy cause without hope of favor or reward."

"Mrs. Weakley and I discussed the matter at length," he remembered, "and despite his plea, we gave him an unqualified no. We tried to explain our reasons for not accepting. To him these reasons did not seem valid, but he reluctantly returned to Birmingham."[4]

Hall and those who commissioned him in Birmingham were not deterred, and he returned to Tennessee three weeks later. "I have come to pray with you and your wife about going to Alabama to head our boys' school," he told the couple. "Mrs. Johnston is also praying in Birmingham that my mission will succeed." Hall spent the evening at the school and told Mr. and Mrs. Weakley more about the institution in Alabama. Weakley admitted that he was impressed by Hall's sincerity but was far from being convinced that he needed to leave the stable situation in Tennessee for the uncertainty of a new and struggling school. However, as Hall left the next morning, Weakley did promise that he and his wife would make it a matter of prayer.

There was no further communication for weeks, then out of nowhere the Weakleys received a letter informing them that the board of directors of the Alabama Boys' Industrial School had elected him as their superintendent and Mrs. Weakley as matron. "We were appointed to jobs which we did not seek and for which we did not apply," Weakley recalled. "We didn't understand it, but felt that we must go. There must have been a greater

Mr. and Mrs. David M. Weakley are shown at the time of their appointment as ABIS's superintendent and matron in 1905.

Power than any human force that guided our decision. Mrs. Johnston said it was the hand of God that brought us. I have never known anyone with so much faith and who so completely relied on Divine guidance as Mrs. Johnston. Surely she walked and talked with God, and she lived in a spiritual atmosphere of confidence and trust that was an inspiration to all those who came in contact with her."

God must have been involved, because there was certainly nothing about the school or the situation at this point that would have been humanly appealing. "Somehow, it never occurred to us to visit the school and look over the situation before we accepted the jobs. Maybe it was providential, for had we done so, I fear we would have returned to Nashville," Weakley admitted. Nevertheless, the couple arrived in Birmingham in late February to look at their new home and place of employment.[5]

Weakley remembered their initial visit in great detail. The couple was met at the train station by Hall and a student named Charlie, "a lanky, sandy-haired boy with beautiful white teeth and an engaging, friendly smile." Their hosts were "driving a beautiful bay mare hitched to a slick looking new surrey with fringe around the top." He would later learn that the surrey was purchased by board members out of their own pockets just for the occasion. With Berta the mare leading the way, the foursome traveled the eight miles to the school in cool, pleasant weather with the remnants of a recent snowfall still covering the ground.[6]

On arrival at the East Lake campus, the students gathered around to size up the husband and wife who would become their new teachers. One precocious boy got right to the point by asking, "Are you the folks what's going to run this school? If you is, I hope you will get us some school books what we can learn."[7]

The youth's spotty grammar pointed to just one of many deficiencies the experienced administrator would notice during his visit. As they surveyed the grounds, they discovered the conditions were quite poor. There was little in the way of landscaping and red mud was everywhere—a sticky nuisance with which Weakley was totally unfamiliar. The words that immediately came to his mind were "devastation, disorder and ruin." He later confessed that during the first evening on campus, they were searching for a way to make a "graceful exit" to return to Nashville, where they had been promised their former positions would be waiting.[8]

The next day, a Sunday, the Lord truly began to work. The Weakleys went with the boys and staff to worship services, which he later described as "simple and impressive with a sincerity of purpose, accompanied by beautiful and tuneful singing."

The afternoon was spent with the boys who had initially impressed him as a "motley, unpromising bunch of unkempt youngsters who cared nothing for the better things of life and who had no ambition for self-improvement." But after a day of mingling and getting to know them on a deeper level, "we found how wrong we were. Their friendly attitude and intelligent questions, and their responsiveness were amazing and we later learned many of them possessed fine minds, were ambitious and eager to learn."

Equally inspiring was the resolve and enlightened attitude of Mrs. Johnston and the board members. Weakley described in some detail the differences in the typical institution of the day and what the women in Birmingham envisioned for their school.

Schools in this era were generally "custodial," Weakley wrote, with "no serious thought given to the individual boy, either to their spiritual, emotional or educational needs. The regulations under which they lived, the training and discipline were often useless and sometimes relentless and cruel. Mrs. Johnston and the Board felt that the Alabama school should be a place that would strengthen and inspire; a home that would prove a blessing and a benediction."

In spite of the difficulties and challenges they saw all around them, there was something drawing the young couple toward this opportunity. Mrs. Weakley summed it up quite simply when she told her husband, "God has sent us to the place." It would be their home and their life's calling for the next forty-three years.[9]

And Johnsie's prayers had been answered again.

8

DWELLING IN GREEN PASTURES

The 136-acre site Mrs. Johnston had found for her new school may have looked right out of the Twenty-third Psalm, but it would take more than green pastures and still waters to accommodate hundreds of delinquent boys. That duty would fall to the board of directors and their capable staff.

Not long after purchasing the initial plot of land, a problem arose, or as Mrs. Johnston would call it, an opportunity. It was discovered that the young man who was an heir of the original seller still owned the adjoining property where the spring that fed the land was located. He was willing to sell, but at age nineteen, he did not have legal standing under Alabama law to enter into the transaction, so Mrs. Johnston went to court to have the young man declared an adult so he could sell the property. Just when things were looking up, a local neighbor came forward to claim that he was part owner of the spring. He, too, was willing to sell, not only his interest in the spring but his property as well, bringing the total acreage to 270 acres. Both new acquisitions were made through donations by the board members and other friends in the community.[1]

The only existing structure on the expansive piece of property, according to the first Superintendent C. D. Griffin, was an "old log cabin, which was filthy, and about to tumble down from old age. We cleaned it up the best we could—whitewashed the walls and scrubbed the floors." This first building was so unsuitable as living quarters that Griffin and his assistant eventually turned it into a dining hall and erected a white tent nearby to serve as a dormitory for the staff and first group of boys.[2] Thus began a construction program that would eventually result in twenty-three buildings erected over the first fifty years of the school's existence.³

Johnston Building

The board immediately authorized construction of a suitable building, completed in late 1900. The board decided on a three-story wooden structure that would sleep seventy-five boys, but also contain school rooms, vocational shops, and other space. The State of Alabama provided only $3,000 for the first year of the school, with more than three times that much in cash and supplies contributed by the community. Most of the labor was donated by local craftsmen.⁴

Birmingham Building

The increase in the student population led to a request for a second building in 1903, which the legislature approved along with another ap-

Johnston Building.

propriation of $3,000 to supplement what the board would raise independently. The building, to be used entirely as a dormitory, was a three-story brick veneer with a slate roof and bell tower. It was very modern for the times, with electric lights, steam heating, and plumbing. When the building was completed, the board requisitioned the $3,000 from the state to pay the balance due, only to be told by the governor that more pressing needs had arisen and the money could not be released. Through Mrs. Johnston's determination, a loan was obtained and disaster averted.[5]

The Campus

Despite Mrs. Johnston's description evoking biblical comparisons, Mr. and Mrs. Weakley would have begged to differ when they arrived in February of 1905. "There were no walks or driveways, only mud, bushes, and briers surrounding all the buildings. Mud holes and ditches were in great profusion." The energetic couple immediately went to work. "We divided

Birmingham Building.

This view shows the campus's first three buildings, as well as the trees planted by Mrs. Weakley. In the foreground is the "ugly gully" that was eventually filled.

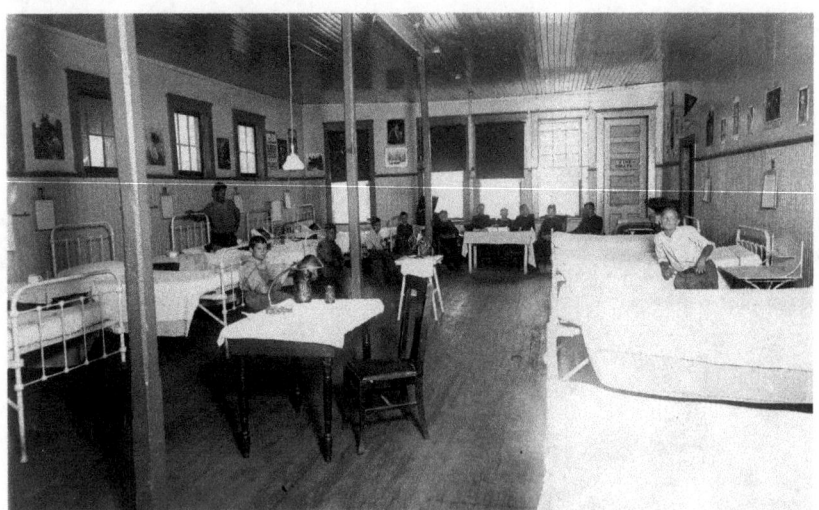

An interior view of one of the early dormitories illustrates the barracks-style accommodations that were common for much of the twentieth century.

Alabama Building, later Johnston Hall.

the boys into work squads, and started to cutting out the underbrush, filling in the low places, and planting grass. We had to do this the hard way by the pick and shovel method. We did not have a wheelbarrow. I begged some lumber from one of my friends who owned a sawmill, and we built a number of plank walks.

"In the Fall of 1905, we started planting shade trees and shrubbery," he continued. "The boys dug these trees from the nearby woods, and in due time, they grew into wonderful shade trees. There were only a few trees on the campus when we arrived, and now there are hundreds of them. When the trees became large enough we had trouble with the boys climbing in them and swinging on the limbs and breaking them off. We solved this problem by having printed on waterproof paper and tacking on each tree the poem 'Trees' by Joyce Kilmer."

Weakley credited his wife with the inspiration and the planning that made the campus into the pastoral setting it eventually became. "Mrs. Weakley assumed the task of beautifying the campus and the result is evidenced today by the beautiful trees and shrubbery. She chose the location of all the buildings and planned for future expansion. Her love for beauty, system and order was one of her outstanding characteristics. If she saw an ugly spot, she would screen it with a rose bush or a climbing vine. Our campus, in due time, compared favorably with that of a well-kept college."[6]

ALABAMA BUILDING/JOHNSTON HALL

The third building on campus, completed in 1907, was the first structure of the Weakley era and also the first paid for entirely by the State of Alabama. It was originally dedicated as the Alabama Building, but was subsequently named Johnston Hall in honor of the school's great lady. The building was three stories of solid brick, with a full basement. The structure was to serve several functions, such as classrooms, staff living quarters, assembly room, kitchen, dining room, and boys' dormitory—a classic example of the congregate plan.

At the turn of the century, there were two schools of thought regarding the layout and operation of a boys' institution. The congregate plan advocated having all of the school's activities under one roof so as to enhance security. This was the method employed by the original House of Refuge in New York and other early institutions. The alternate approach was called the cottage system, which called for housing the boys in smaller cottages, with functions such as the academics, dining, vocational shops, and the like being located in separate buildings. Over time, ABIS would transition to such a system.

At the time the structure was raised, funds were insufficient to excavate and finish the basement. In anticipation of doing this at a later date, the walls were built to the proper height that would allow the boys to dig up the dirt and roll it out in wheelbarrows; the carpentry shop would then complete the interior. As this process got underway, a major obstacle was encountered. A huge limestone rock twelve by ten by eight feet was unearthed—much too large to go through the basement door. Attempts to break it apart with sledge hammers and steel chisels proved fruitless. The only alternative appeared to be blasting powder, which could possibly damage the foundation of the massive building.

Engineers and contractors were discussing their limited options when a barefooted boy who had been observing the proceedings interrupted their conversation.

"Mister, if that was my rock, I'd tell you what I'd do."

"Son, what would you do?" the engineer asked kindly.

"Well, sir," the boy replied, "I'd come right alongside of this rock and I'd dig a hole big enough to put the rock in, and after I'd hauled out the dirt, I'd prize the rock in the hole and cover it up."

After some consultation with his colleagues, the professional engineer acknowledged the common-sense approach of his young amateur colleague, and that was exactly what was done.[7]

Shop Building

The next major project at the campus was a three-story wooden building to be used exclusively as a shop for all of the vocational programs. The state was unable to make any appropriations, and there were insufficient internal funds to hire an architect or laborers, so the carpentry instructor designed the building and the boys did all the work. Practically every vocational department at the school was involved in one way or another, and the boys pitched in willingly as they realized the resulting facility would be for their own benefit. The first floor housed the printing, barbering, plumbing, electrical, auto repair, and machine shops, while the second floor held carpentry, tailoring, the shoe shop, and band room. The third floor was reserved for storage.[8]

Kilby Hall

Kilby Hall was a two-story, brick dormitory built in 1921. Rather than the large, barracks-style rooms found in some of the other dorms, this building had small rooms for three boys each. The woodworking shop made the furniture, and the student paint crew decorated the rooms in pastel colors, making the interior homelike and attractive. Hot and cold water was available in each room.[9]

BUSH CHAPEL

One of the most impressive of the early buildings was the Bush Chapel, built in 1923. The money for this place of worship was donated by long-time board member and treasurer, Mrs. T. G. Bush. Weakley described it as being of "colonial architecture, simple in beauty, classical in design, and presenting a picture of spiritual restfulness." A bronze plaque was placed over the entrance of the 500-seat sanctuary proclaiming "those that seek me early shall find me."

The Bush Chapel is one of the few remaining buildings from the early days of the campus. The family assumed the responsibility of preserving and maintaining the chapel upon Mrs. Bush's death in 1930.[10]

McLESTER HALL

Another dormitory was added in the late 1920s. The two-story edifice had rooms that accommodated four boys, with built-in beds, lockers, and study desks for each boy made by the woodworking class. The first floor contained a living room and space for recreation and hobbies.[11]

MECHANIC ARTS BUILDING

This vocational building, also added in the late 1920s, replaced the original wooden shop built twenty-five years earlier. The older boys helped with the construction of the facility, with one crew working in the morning while another attended academic classes and the two groups exchanging places in the afternoon. The two-story brick structure was designed in the shape of a "T" and contained space for eight trades on the ground floor and six trades, plus storage, on the second floor.[12]

CRAIGHEAD HALL

Craighead Hall was built in 1932 with assistance from President Franklin Roosevelt's Works Progress Administration (WPA) to serve as a kitchen and dining hall, with special accommodations for staff and guests. The boys' contributions to this endeavor consisted of making venetian blinds for the windows and doing all of the painting. The building was named for long-time board member Mrs. Erwin Craighead.[13]

Little Mount Vernon

Throughout most of Mrs. Johnston's adult life she had one other consuming passion in addition to the beloved school for her boys. Mrs. Johnston was an ardent admirer of George Washington. She became involved with the Mount Vernon Association and later served as a board member and regent of the organization. An avid collector of relics pertaining to the nation's first president, she later helped retrieve articles that belonged in his home.

In the early 1930s, the Highland Book Club built Mrs. Johnston a cottage on the grounds of the school, and she dubbed it Little Mount Vernon. It became a place where she could spend her last days in the company of her boys. The students made her a four-poster bed that was a replica of President Washington's, and a set of draperies in the cottage actually came from Washington's home. A mirror that adorned a wall in the cottage was made from a walnut tree on the Virginia estate, and many of the plants in her garden came from Mount Vernon.

After Mrs. Johnston's death, Little Mount Vernon continued to serve the school in numerous ways, including several years as the library.[14]

Adele Goodwyn McNeel School

This academic building of the late 1930s was named for Mrs. McNeel to recognize her contributions as board president succeeding Mrs. Johnston. The brick facility contained twelve classrooms, a library, and special rooms for art, music, and handicrafts. The structure also contained a 500-seat auditorium, complete with a "moving picture projector."[15]

Weakley Hall

Weakley Hall was built in 1940 with the assistance of the WPA as another dormitory. Each of the nine bedrooms on the second floor housed four boys, with a lavatory, bed, locker, and writing table for each one. The first floor was devoted to a living room and recreation and bathroom facilities. Once again, the students lent a hand with the painting, furniture, and even the curtains.[16]

Underwood Hall

This final building project of the Weakley era was another dormitory built on the same general plan as McLester and Weakley halls, although somewhat smaller with seven bedrooms for four boys each. The building, constructed during the administration of Governor Chauncey Sparks, 1943–47, was named for Mrs. John Lewis Underwood, another deserving board member. In a fitting epilogue to this chapter on the growth of the campus, it is interesting to note how much construction costs and property values had risen in fifty years. The first biennial report indicated that the total value of the property and the one building at the end of 1900 was about $18,000. The construction and furnishing of Underwood Hall alone was close to $100,000.[17]

9

An Open Door

In a 1948 *Birmingham Post-Herald* article, writer Jane Aldridge admitted to being a little confused about the boys' institution on the outskirts of the city. "It's far easier to tell what the Alabama Boys' Industrial School 'is not' than to attempt to describe what it really is," she declared. "It is not, for instance, a reform school. Not if by reform school you mean, as most people do, a sort of 'junior penitentiary.' You begin to realize this distinction," she continued, "as you approach the school and notice that there is no fence around the grounds. No gates to pass through or guards to want to know what your business is . . . Though every boy is there by court order, and a few have been accused of very serious crimes, even grand larceny and murder, you'll not find an iron bar at a single window."

What the reporter did find was the complete opposite. "Instead, you see normal happy-looking boys, strolling casually over a lovely campus that would do credit to a fine prep school. They laugh and talk as they walk. Some romp there in the yard with dogs that have taken up at the school and have been adopted as pets by the boys. Others, their chores and lessons completed, play softball."[1]

Founder Elizabeth Johnston undoubtedly would have beamed at such a description. That is exactly what she and her all-female board of directors envisioned when they organized the school some fifty years earlier.

The innovative practice was first mentioned by Mrs. Johnston in her report to the governor in January 1905. The board president was commenting on the new leadership at the institution and the changes they were implementing.

"Mr. and Mrs. Connelley were appointed to succeed Mr. and Mrs. Griffin, coming to the work without previous training and when everything was in a state of unrest and confusion," she related. "Their success [1904–05] has been wonderful and I feel we owe them our safe passage through some very troubled waters."

"Among other reforms, they have adopted the 'Open Door System,' which seems to have been very successful," she said of her new team. "The superintendent of a similar institution said 'he had high walls around his school' and expressed great surprise that we could hold the boys at all, when they were allowed such liberty.

"Mr. Connelley's efforts are to make the boy strong enough to resist temptation and to develop his sense of honor," she said. "One practical result of this plan was that the boys went into the neighboring fields, with no guard except the boy in command of the squad, and picked cotton for which they received one hundred and twenty-five dollars."[2]

When David Weakley was hired the following year as the new superintendent, Mrs. Johnston could not have found a more enthusiastic ally. Weakley's personality, experience, and philosophy were a perfect fit for this enlightened form of correctional administration. In his first report to his new employers, he goes into great detail in discussing his view of the institution.

"There appears to be a prevailing mistaken idea among the public in general as to the nature of the work and the kind of men we produce," he explained. "There are some who persist in clinging to the antiquated and erroneous belief that the School is a horrid place of detention—a young penal institution with cross-barred windows and ominous frowning walls of detention which are a perpetual reminder to the hard, awful, crime-visaged jailbird that he is a prisoner.

"The Alabama Boy's Industrial School is not a prison, nor is it a penal institution in any form, where erring boys are confined and cruel punishment unjustly meted out to them," he informed his readers. "Neither is it a place of confinement where they put bad boys to keep them out of other people's way."

The young superintendent then gave the board the contrasting picture of the open-door system. "Our methods of keeping the boys are simple. We have no armed guards as some believe; we have no bolts or bars to keep them from running away—not even a fence. To retain the boys, we must show them by example and precept that we are interested in their future position as good citizens of the state, and much concerned about their spiritual welfare. Win their confidence, good will, and that best and strongest of all ties—love."[3]

After his second year at the helm, Weakley was even more emphatic about the school's new strategy. "The 'Open Door' experiment is no longer a theory, but a proven reality and has come to stay, but it never ceases to be a source of wonder to visitors from a distance, and our friends over the State marvel how it is that we manage to keep boys whom they regard as the worst element possible without the aid of bolts, bars and a high wall. Boys do sometimes run away from us, but they sometimes run away from home; in fact, many of them are here for that very reason."[4]

For Weakley, the open door policy also meant that his office and his heart were always open for his students and their problems. There are numerous stories that demonstrate the attitude of the kindly administrator and the warm feelings he had for "his boys."

One day Weakley had a conversation with a fleet-footed student who was continually using the school's lack of security to his advantage. "Archibald, why do you insist on running away?" Weakley asked.

'Well, sir," the little boy replied, "every now and then I just feel like I gotta go, and . . . well, I gotta go."

"Well, I'll tell you, Archibald." Weakley nodded as he looked down at the youngster. "Sometimes I feel that way myself. Next time you feel like you gotta go, come tell me and we'll run away together."

About three weeks passed, when suddenly the habitual runner burst into the superintendent's office. "Colonel,[*] I gotta go!" he said excitedly.

The colonel calmly got up from his desk, retrieved his hat, and the pair left. For half a day they roamed the woods near the campus, and even stopped to do some fishing with some make-shift line the colonel just happened to have in his pocket. After an hour of fishing, Archibald looked up and said, "Well, Colonel, I'm ready to go back."

---

[*] As a consequence of the Alabama National Guard's annual review of ABIS's military program, David Weakley was commissioned an honorary colonel of infantry in service of the State of Alabama. Most of the boys at the school referred to Superintendent Weakley as "Colonel."

David Weakley may have had a military bearing, but there was true compassion behind the façade. His open door policy went against the norm found in most reform schools of the era.

"That's funny," said Weakley. "So am I." The two friends walked back together, and little Archibald never ran away again.[5]

Weakley also delighted in telling about the time a colleague from another state visited the school. The colonel was showing his guest around the campus when they came upon a group of boys who were cutting a watermelon. "Colonel Weakley," the boys waved. "Wouldn't you like a piece of melon, too?" The visitor was shocked and curtly said that at his school a boy would never address the superintendent without first being granted permission to speak.[6]

Another example of Weakley's homespun way of handling troubled youngsters is shown by his dealings with a boy named Joe. His mother had brought him to the school because he was always fighting. When he arrived, his mother had him decked out in a ruffled shirt, short pants, tan shoes, and stockings. Atop his head was a flat, white straw hat adorned with tassels. Weakley referred to it as a Little Lord Fauntleroy suit.

"Joe, we don't have any fighting at the school," Weakley told him. "I'll do all the fighting from now on." The boy left the office to begin his stay at the school. Within thirty minutes he was back for nearly drowning a much larger boy in the spring near the campus.

"Joe, what happened?" Weakley inquired.

"He laughed at my suit and said I was a sissy," the boy said in his defense.

"Joe, we are going to get rid of that Fauntleroy suit," Weakley concluded.

From that point forward, Joe's wardrobe at the school consisted of a pair of baggy overalls, an old frayed palmetto hat, and bare feet. He never had any more trouble fighting and was soon released from the school. Weakley was correct that the problem was all "in the breeches." Joe later became a highway patrolman.[7]

The Archibalds and Joes aside, all situations could not be resolved that easily, especially in the latter stages of Weakley's tenure. In the 1930–31 fiscal year, with a population of 450 students, the institution had a total of 129 escapes. Even Weakley recognized that times were changing.[8]

In his 1945 report to the board he stated, "We operate on the open door plan. We allow our boys more freedom than is usually permitted in similar institutions. We think it is more effective to put the boys on their honor than it would be to deprive them of their freedom. "Delinquency is increasing in intensity, however, and some of the boys are harder to control," he admitted. "Their delinquencies are serious and deep-rooted. If this continues, we may have to build a detention unit where this type of boy can be segregated until such a time he can be safely allowed to associate with others."[9]

The Alabama Boys' Industrial School, however, went against the norm longer than most institutions of its kind. Due in large measure to the legacies of Johnston and Weakley, the school did not surround its campus with a fence until nearly a century after its founding.[10]

10

AN HONEST TRADE

Everyone has heard the old adage about idleness being the devil's workshop. That was not a problem at the new school for wayward boys. The Alabama Boys' Industrial School had a few workshops of its own to provide instruction in a vocation as well as life.

The founders of the school did not choose the word "industrial" lightly. From a meager beginning of four trades, the school eventually reached a peak of nearly twenty different vocations in which they offered training.[1] Unlike some of the nation's early institutions for delinquent and destitute boys that forced their residents to work at menial tasks as a means of punishment, the Alabama Boys' Industrial School from the beginning seems to have placed its emphasis on rehabilitation rather than retaliation.

"Every thoughtful citizen must agree," Mrs. Johnston wrote the governor in the school's first annual report, "that it is a duty the State owes its wayward and criminally disposed boys to remove them from temptation and inspire them with hope, whilst training brain and hand, rather than punish them by association and contact with our worst criminals and hand them over to predestinated destruction."[2]

The able board president then went on to relate a sad and dramatic tale that spoke volumes about the plight of many of the state's at-risk boys, and the government's responsibility to act.

"The children themselves have an instinctive sense of this obligation on the part of the State. It is related that when a boy was on the way to the scaffold to be executed for a capital felony, he turned to the minister present and in piteous tones exclaimed: 'Mister! O, Mister! Tell them I ain't had no chance, no how!' This should never be uttered by a boy of Alabama again."[3]

In giving the youngsters under his care the opportunity for which the boy pleaded, Superintendent C. D. Griffin took a practical, two-fold approach to the value of industrial training. In modern correctional parlance, he saw its benefits in terms of both managing the boys while in the institution and providing them a future upon release.

"We need more room, more industries and better equipment for these we have already established," he wrote. "An idle brain is the devil's workshop and while we give the boys play hours, we make them work and study in due proportion. Our aim is to prepare them at the Industrial school for supporting themselves by an honest trade when they are turned out into the world."[4]

Early records indicate that printing, carpentry, blacksmithing, and leatherworking were the first skills selected toward that end.

PRINTING

"We have tried to equip the Printing Department with first-class, up-to-date appliances for printing," Griffin reported at the end of his first year. With this fledgling effort, the school's industrial program was underway. He further mentioned that the printing operation had been most helpful in producing letterheads, envelopes, and even a school newspaper.

"We have a paper started which we call the *Boys' Banner*. It has been cordially received by institution papers throughout the United State and we have quite a large exchange list. We have had a great many complimentary notices from superintendents of various schools, for it is a rare thing to start a paper within the first year of the school's existence."[5] This student-produced periodical would be a staple of the institution for fifty years.

In Griffin's next report, printing appears to have suffered the growing pains associated with the entire institution.

"The printing department has been kept up all the year and our magazine used, but not as promptly as we would like, as we have had so little help and so much to attend to that some duties have been more or less neglected."[6]

When Colonel Weakley assumed the helm of the school, the printing department received an infusion of new blood—and more ink.

"The printing office is one of the most interesting and at the same time one of the most useful shops on the place," Weakley related. "About an

The ABIS print shop provided training for the boys and published the school newspaper.

average number of 12 boys, under a competent instructor, are given daily lessons four and one-half hours in typesetting, color work, job and press work, besides acquiring practical experience in the newspaper line."

During this period the school newspaper continued to grow. "This department produces semi-monthly a small twelve-page periodical, *The Boys' Banner*, which is distributed among the children and friends of the institution; it also brings to us many bright, newsy exchanges, which the boys delight to read." Over the years, the *The Banner* would evolve into a monthly and later a weekly publication.

Apparently Weakley did not find the department's printing equipment in quite the pristine condition that his predecessor had boasted only three years earlier. "Our press, an old second-hand affair, is in very bad shape and should be replaced by a new one or rebuilt at the factory," he lamented. "The face of some of the type is completely worn out and is no good whatever, except as old metal. It will cost about $500 to put this department in first-class working order."⁷

The school was fortunate during Weakley's years to receive donations of printing equipment from the *Birmingham News* and *Birmingham Age-Herald*, as well as special appropriations from governors Thomas Kilby and Bibb Graves. On occasion, equipment was donated by national companies that specialized in making printing presses. Weakley commented that when the school had an opportunity to get equipment, it always sought to get that which would make the boys most marketable. His thinking was sound, for most of the students left the school with jobs in hand at local newspapers, and a few with the Government Printing Office in Washington, D.C.⁸

As the school grew and perfected its training, the scope of the printing operation expanded as well. In addition to letterheads, envelopes, and the like, the printing class eventually began producing all the forms and documents used by the school's academic department and hospital, as well as all of the school's promotional literature and the annual report.

In the school's twenty-fifth annual report, Weakley even suggested that with a little more support in funding and equipment, the operation would be able to assist the State of Alabama in some of its overall printing needs.⁹ Not bad for what started as a handful of teenagers with ink smudges on their fingers and faces.

Carpentry

In the formative years of the Alabama Boys' Industrial School, carpentry—or its variations—was probably the most useful of all the trades, as the boys literally built the institution around themselves.

"We have a few cheap tools and with these some of our boys have made excellent progress in the art of carpentry," C. D. Griffin wrote in his report for 1901–02. "An engine house, a large outhouse, green house, tables for the dining room, and numerous shelves, doors, and cupboards can be exhibited at the school.

"With our new scroll saw, a Christmas present, we hope to have a collection of finer work to exhibit next year. The boys are interested in wood carving. I have bought a set of carving tools and hope to show some work

Furniture made in the school's carpentry shop awaits placement in one of the dormitories. The various shops on campus helped the school become very self-sufficient in its operations.

in our paper before long of their making," the first superintendent stated.[10]

As with most of the trades, carpentry made rapid strides with the arrival of Colonel Weakley who was himself a former instructor in this skill. He went to great lengths in his first report to discuss its intricacies and its benefits. Although most carpenters certainly appreciate the skills required of their work, probably few have ever described their work as eloquently as did Weakley:

"Manual Training, or Sloyd, is any form of constructive work that serves to develop the powers of the pupil through spontaneous and intelligent self-activity," he explained. "Sloyd is truly a constructive work; the pupils are taught after they have made a perfect mechanical drawing of the object they wish to produce, that it must be constructed according to strict specifications which are shown on their drawing—not too long or too short—but just right, with no imperfection of any kind. By means of drawing, sawing, planning, etc., the pupils are taught to become skillful with their hands, patient, accurate, clean, careful, persistent and persevering;

A set of table and chairs made by James Dawsey's carpentry students is ready to be moved into the dining hall.

thereby strengthening the brain through the medium of touch and sight, at the same time cultivating a respect, love and value of rough labor."

Weakley went on to explain to the uninformed reader the depth of the training that would be provided the novice carpenters. "No set of models has to our knowledge been designed that express the complete idea of manual training," he wrote. "Therefore, while we are operating this department which we deem so essential, we shall use freely the best ideas found in the Swedish, German, Russian and American courses as the basis of our teaching, at the same time reserving the right to draw from our own originality . . ."[11]

To begin his pupils' training, Weakley acquired through donated funds the tools to furnish twelve regulation work benches, featuring drawing boards, planes, saws, hammers, braces, bits, and other tools. Later, with appropriations from the Kilby administration, power tools such as sanders, band saws, drill presses, and the like were added. The school even had a machine to make its own brooms and brushes, and the school farm grew the broom corn to supply the bristles.

As the size and skill level of the carpentry class increased, the boys took on greater challenges. Their first projects were a shed and barn for the farm, and later the boys erected the vocational program's first shop building in 1910. Over the years, the boys would have a hand in the constructing most of the buildings on the growing campus. Eventually, the class made all the furnishings for the buildings, including beds, chests, tables, chairs, and desks. As noted earlier, the boys even made venetian blinds.[12]

The evolution of the carpentry and woodworking shop is embodied in the life of James Dawsey. He was a student at the school in the early 1900s, and after serving in World War I, came back to serve as the carpentry/woodworking instructor. Dawsey's grandson, Scott, provided the details of this lifelong love affair with the school:

> As a boy, my grandfather was very artistic, He could take a piece of wood and make anything out of it. He decided he was going to make a

James Dawsey (far left) and two friends while students at ABIS. Dawsey later returned as the carpentry instructor and remained on staff for 47 years.

covered wagon. So, he went down and bought all the stuff at the hardware store to make a covered wagon and he charged it to his daddy and made his daddy mad. Now, his daddy was in the State Legislature at the time, so I guess Mrs. Johnston had been with the Legislature trying to get funding and he knew about the school. So, he sent him there. It was just silly, silly, silly. When my grandfather went, he was going to stay for a few months or a year maybe—that's what they intended to send him down there for just to straighten him up. But he didn't want to come home; he loved it. Mrs. Johnston was a mother to those guys. They loved Mrs. Johnston.

Like many of the boys, James Dawsey left the school to enter World War I. Upon his return to Alabama after the war, he received a letter from an old ABIS friend. Scott Dawsey said:

Lonnie A. was a classmate there with my grandfather, and he later

James Dawsey sits at his desk late in his forty-seven year career as ABIS carpentry instructor.

became a teacher there; he was in charge of one of the military companies and ran one of the shops. Lonnie sent him this letter in 1919 in Hartford, where my grandfather's family home was, telling him how great things are, telling him the pay is better, and that they've got biscuits every morning. He tells him you need to come back up here. So, he goes back up there and he stays 47 years.[13]

Colonel Weakley would have been the superintendent at the time that young James Dawsey was sent there for the covered wagon fiasco. Weakley and Mrs. Johnston always had a soft spot for any of "their boys" and nothing made them prouder than for one of them to come "home" to work at the institution. This is clearly evident years later when Weakley wrote of Dawsey's tenure at the school and his ability to shape more than just wood.

"James Dawsey is a capable and dedicated person who sets a high standard of excellence on the work of the boys," Weakley said of his former student turned faculty member. "He is especially gifted in designing beautiful carved art pieces that were a surprise to all those who saw them, and they wondered how boys could be taught to produce such delicate and exquisite work. This instructor has been with the school for a long number of years. He has never faltered in his work, and his interest in the welfare of his pupils has grown throughout the years. They come to visit him from far-away places and they write to him from foreign lands.

"His greatest work has not been with material things, but that he has been able to instill in the hearts and minds of hundreds of boys a sincere purpose and a feeling of confidence that has enabled them to become qualified to go out and face the world unafraid."[14]

Blacksmithing

No other trade at the Alabama Boys' Industrial School conveyed the feelings of the era in which the school was established than the blacksmith shop. These were the days of the horse and buggy, and there were horses to be shod and buggy axles and wagon wheels to be repaired. The blacksmith shop began as a necessity to curtail expenses but evolved into a training opportunity.

"The latter part of April, we purchased and installed a set of blacksmith tools consisting of forge, anvil, tongs, stocks, dies, etc. which have proved a saving and a valuable addition to the school," Colonel Weakley related in his report for 1905. "Heretofore, when we wished a bolt or a wagon repaired, or a plow point sharpened, we were forced to make a trip to East Lake, not only paying for the work done, but losing valuable time from our farm.

"The blacksmith shop has amply demonstrated its usefulness," he continued, "and if we can secure the means, we hope in the near future to employ a regular class in forge work and horse shoeing."[15]

In short order, that hope was realized, as Weakley remembered in his personal papers. "We decided to start a shop and were able to secure as instructor a man of long experience in the trade. He was a person of excellent character, an outstanding workman; in fact, he was an artist in shaping, welding, and designing beautiful and useful articles constructed of wrought iron. As usual, it was a question of money, but after talking the matter over with Mr. B. F. Moore, President of Moore and Handley Hardware Company, to my surprise he said he would like to donate the major part of the equipment, which consisted of two anvils, forge, hammers, tongs, etc.

"We built a makeshift shop . . . under a beautiful spreading elm tree. In weeks we assigned six boys to learn the trade, and we were in the blacksmith business," the superintendent explained. "The instructor was pleased with the setup, and the boys were elated, and their progress was rapid. We were able to keep our farm equipment in excellent condition, put shoes on the mules, and besides making needed repairs, the instructor taught the boys to make gate hinges and fasteners and such articles as fire tongs, pokers and shovels. Later, they made two complete two-horse wagons. They were neatly appointed, and had the appearance of being factory-made. We used them for years."[16]

Henry Ford and the progress that rode in with his Model-T eventually made the blacksmith shop obsolete. "As time passed, and the use of the automobile increased, the need for the blacksmith shop also passed," Weakley admitted, "so, we converted the blacksmith shop into an automobile repair shop. Here again, our friends came to our aid and donated several automobiles. This was a move in the right direction, and during the years, we have been able to run out many a good workman."[17]

Shoe Shop

For most of the Huck Finns at the school, new shoes were a luxury, but it was one to which they soon became accustomed.

"We have a poorly equipped shop, but the boys have learned to do some very nice work," C. D. Griffin wrote of one of the school's first trades. "We are making some new shoes, keep our old ones well repaired, which saves us much expense. Of course, most of our boys are barefoot during the summer.

"We have also commenced making harness with our limited facilities and we have repaired our harness and have made several bridles. Considering that these boys have never done any work before to amount to anything and now are able to do this work, it shows we are doing something toward making industrious citizens out of raw material."[18]

The following year, Griffin's report showed continued progress in this class. "During the summer we put in a supply of lasts, patterns, and tools for the making of shoes," he wrote. "We found an old second-hand sewing machine, which we could afford to buy, and now the boys in the shoe shop are making some excellent shoes, which out-wear the shoes we buy, and do not cost as much and teaches the boys in the department a good trade."[19]

During Colonel Weakley's early years at the school, a situation occurred that is indicative of how things were done until the new institution could gain its financial footing. "One day I heard there was a small shoe manufacturing plant in Birmingham that had failed in business and was being sold at auction," he related in his papers. "I inspected this machinery and found six or eight factory machines in excellent condition that I knew we could use to advantage. I bid them in at less than $400, but after I had bought them I realized I did not have the money, so I rushed to the people who sold us our groceries and asked if I could borrow this amount. They were very obliging and we used this machinery for a long number of years to great advantage. We were able to make our shoes in a more or less professional manner and more rapidly. The product turned out not only useful, but nice looking."[20]

In his 1915 report, Weakley made the following assessment of the shoe shop. "The shoe shop, under a competent instructor—one of our own students—has done excellent work: 635 pairs of shoes, worth $2.25 each, have been made, 3099 soles put on old shoes, 2035 heels repaired and put on, and 1116 patches applied.[21]

By most accounts all of this work was done with approximately ten students placed in the shoe shop. That's a lot of soles for ten young souls. Perhaps the explanation is found in a 1931 report by the instructor, Don Smith. "Most of the boys like the shop and work to learn all they can, and to be sure, they are looking forward to the time when he can go to his home town and obtain work for himself. I have three boys who are ready for jobs, and they appreciate the fact that the institution has helped them to get ready for their vocation. These boys are very enthusiastic."[22]

Whether it was wood, leather, or boys, the school seemed to have a knack for turning raw materials into useful products.

11

The Junk Heap

As the Weakley era gained a firm footing, more industries and trades were added to the school's curriculum. Weakley explained the rationale for this expansion in one of his annual reports to the board. "Practically all our boys will have to make a living with their hands," Weakley told the board. "If they are taught to do this, we must provide for them a more varied and extensive program. They need, in addition to their regular school work, superior, intensive training in creative handicrafts, suitable to their abilities."[1]

With this idea in mind, Weakley and his staff developed an application and assessment process for their industrial program. Each boy was given a choice of a trade, but his decision was supplemented by a tryout period and, as they became available, aptitude tests. Once this evaluation was completed, the staff would move a boy to another trade if they determined it was more suitable to the boy's talents. Upon completion of a specific vocational class, the student was presented a framed "certificate of apprenticeship," and exceptional graduates were also given a "certificate of appreciation." Certain meritorious learners received a small salary as a reward for their outstanding work.[2]

Tailoring and Sewing

A sewing shop was added to the list of industries sometime within the first five years of the school. According to one of the early reports to the board, many of the smaller boys were placed in this shop and received four and a half hours of instruction each day. In the early years, the shop produced shirts, pants, sheets, pillow cases, and napkins.[3] By 1915, the apparel had grown to include overalls, military uniforms, underwear, nightgowns, belts, caps, and a mysterious item that Weakley called "easy-walkers," probably an early version of the bedroom slipper or house shoe. In addition to the making of new garments, the shop also stayed busy with mending and patching. In 1915, the boys mended or applied patches to 13,600 items. Ten years later, that number had grown to 27,449 items.[4]

The sewing and tailoring operation would never have reached such heights without the help—once again—of a loyal friend. Just a few months after Weakley purchased some machinery for the shoe shop with an advance from the local grocer, the prudent superintendent found himself at another auction putting in a bid of $300 on eight Singer sewing machines. Just as before, Weakley's bid was the winner, and he was forced to rush down to the market a second time for a loan. One could imagine that this grocer might cringe each time he saw Weakley running toward his business, except for the fact that the headmaster was always faithful to settle his debts.

Like those in the other trades, many of the graduates in sewing and tailoring went on to have careers in the business. Even if they moved into other occupations along the way, the acquired skills still paid off. According to Weakley, one alumnus of the class paid his way through college by doing mending, altering, and ironing for his friends.[5]

Painting

The paint shop began in a lean-to constructed by the boys and their instructors and grew to be one of the school's most beneficial trades for the students and the campus.

Many of today's experts in correctional treatment speak of the value that color can have on a youngster's mood and temperament. In his uncanny way, Weakley may have realized this years before it became accepted practice.

"This work appealed to the boys," Weakley said in his papers, "and soon the whole place took on a bright and cheery appearance. We found most of the boys in the school were partial to brilliant colors and would ask that their dormitories be painted in some outlandish colors, but we tried to grant their request if feasible."[6]

The boys' talents and labors were quite useful to the school as well. In the 1931 report, the shop instructor indicated that the boys had painted the hospital, the steps and reception room of Johnston Hall, the classrooms in the Alabama Building, the officers' mess hall, and the second floor of Kilby Hall.[7]

The boys took their talents all over the state upon release, and often added a previously hidden flair. Weakley told of a visit to Dothan in which he ran into one of the school's former students. The young man simply had to show his father-figure some of his handiwork and escorted Weakley down the street to a Greek restaurant that he had decorated and painted.[8]

BAKERY

Boys have just got to eat, and those working in the bakery helped with that enormous task in the face of daunting obstacles.

In 1931, the instructor was proud of the accomplishments of the boys, but obviously dispirited over the conditions in which they toiled. "At the end of another year we are still in an old place, but it is in a little better condition now than it was a year ago, yet it is far from being an ideal place for a bakery. We have had a hard year's work with more boys to feed and all the old boys gone home or transferred to other places and having to use new boys. They have all done fine and take great interest in their work. We are still hoping for a new bakery."

A listing of the items prepared that year provides some indication of the appetite of that many boys—and to the size of their collective sweet tooth. The boys prepared more than 600,000 buns, but they also turned out 7,550 pies, 2,362 dozen cupcakes, 324 layer cakes, 260 pound cakes, 175 fruit cakes, and 1,245 dozen cinnamon rolls![9]

It is no wonder that the school also had a thriving dental office.

BARBERING

An old ditty from the early 1900s popularized the refrain "Shave and a haircut—two bits." At that rate, it is not difficult to see the value of the barbering class at a boys' school.

"We really have no suitable room for a barber shop," lamented the instructor in 1925. "The uninitiated would not know the value of a shop in a school like ours and just how necessary it is. I hope before the end of the present year to find some place for the shop and equip it in a sanitary and up-to-date manner, so the boys will really have a chance to learn the trade in a satisfactory way."[10]

Apparently, the desired upgrade was completed in 1931. "The barber shop has changed its location since our last annual report... We are proud of our new shop. We are not asking for very much equipment this time, but we really do need three pair of barber shears, three razors and an electric clipper.

"An average of eight boys worked in this shop daily. They have been taught a great deal about barber work, but we could not recommend them for a public shop as they have had experience only with work on men and boys."

As for the savings to the taxpayers of Alabama? At two bits—or 25 cents—a head? "We feel this department has accomplished quite a bit of work, as the monthly reports show there were 8,095 hair cuts and 2,795 shaves during the year."[11]

Sheet Metal

The sheet metal shop was taught by longtime band director Eugene Jordan and was also filled with a number of band members. Part of this connection may have stemmed from the fact that occasional repairs may have been required on some of the band's instruments, and it simply grew from there.

As the boys' skills increased, the articles made and repaired certainly extended beyond clarinets and trumpets. According to various reports submitted by Weakley and Jordan, the list included washboards, stove pipes, milk buckets for the dairy, pans for the kitchen, dippers for the water buckets, toilets, and sinks.

Some of the metal used in their projects came from the local junkyard, and according to Weakley, the sheriff often brought the shop the copper he recovered from the moonshine stills he destroyed.[12]

Machine Shop

According to Weakley, the machine shop may have been the most popular trade on campus, and the reasons behind it are no different than might be cited today.

"Most boys like to see wheels moving and they are fascinated by seeing sparks flying from the grinding machines and red hot shavings from the lathes," Weakley explained. "We have always had more applicants for the machinist trade than any other."[13]

In his 1931 report, instructor H. C. Wood detailed the nature of the work and the required curriculum. "They are first tried in the tool room for a few months and are advanced according to their ability. A series of jobs is given to the new boy, such as chipping and filing, before he is placed on a machine. He is then placed on the shaper for a series of jobs, then to the drill press, then to the lathe or milling machine, depending a great deal on his ability." Wood also described the importance of mathematics, mechanical drawing, and safety in the instruction.[14]

As the modern innovations of the twentieth century began to modernize the life of the average American, the types of trades offered by the Alabama Boys' Industrial School also changed. Automobile mechanics, electrical training, plumbing, and radio repair were added to the curriculum to replace those whose usefulness had passed.

With all of these changes, one staple would remain in all of the classes, however, and that was the school's emphasis on self-reliance. "Like most schools and people, we were always impoverished for lack of funds, but poverty of material things is not too bad if one does not develop a poverty of the spirit," Weakley stated. "With this in mind, we tried to teach our boys to take the things they have and make the best of it . . . We almost lived in the junk yards for there we found at a price we could pay many things the boys could repair and we needed. This experience was good for them and provided an avenue of training and valuable lessons of economy."

Colonel Weakley then broadened his thoughts on reclamation to include the more significant issue of discarded lives. "Junk yards are somewhat like people," he concluded. "There are many on humanity's junk heap who can be reclaimed to a life of usefulness if they can only receive a helping hand."[15]

12

Down on the Farm

One of the obstacles faced by the board and staff of the Alabama Boys' Industrial School can—with all due respects to Paris—be summed up by the question: "How are you going to keep them down on the farm after they've seen Birmingham?"

This was not a problem unique to the new school located on 270 acres of land in eastern Jefferson County. Other administrators around the country were facing the same issue, especially with the trend in juvenile corrections moving away from large, punitive, prison-like institutions toward industrial school campuses located on expansive farms.

Hastings Hornell Hart, one of the leading criminologists and social workers of the early twentieth century, predicted this dilemma in one of his books. He believed that farm life was ideal for building the character of many boys, calling it a "wholesome and happy life." At the same time, however, he admitted that "only a minority of boys in juvenile reformatories can be adapted to life on the farm." Hart contended that "the majority of boys come from the cities and villages; they have the town fever in their veins and it is almost impossible to keep them on the farms. It is true also that many country boys crave the town life."[1]

It was with these challenges that the Alabama Boy's Industrial School began its industrial farm in June 1900. Their only farm-related assets the first year were one pair of mules, a harness, plows, assorted tools, two registered Jerseys, two registered Devons, two Cotswold sheep, and Berkshire and Victoria pigs. The total value was estimated at $633.[2]

The first year or so was devoted primarily to meeting the basic needs of the boys and staff. "Our table was supplied both of the past summers with a variety of vegetables," C. D. Griffin wrote. "We also saved a quantity of turnips, potatoes, beets and peas for winter use. Several barrels of cucumbers were put in brine for pickles, and gallons of tomatoes, blackberries and plums were canned."

The boys also hired out to make extra money. "One of our neighbors employed us to assist in picking cotton, and although few of the boys were acquainted with this form of labor, they soon became very skillful," the superintendent wrote. "The first summer we earned $35.80, which we invested in cutlery for the school. This past summer we again picked cotton and earned $36.85, which we expended for a large rectangular clock for our reception hall to be inscribed 'Presented to the Boys' Industrial School by the boys of 1902.'"[3]

The first actual farm manager, C. M. Taul, described what he faced when he took the job in 1904. "I found it in a rather bad condition, without suitable tools and the stock to properly work the place. Briars, bushes, and crabgrass were in profusion, and caused us to have a great deal of extra work that ought to have been done years before."

A group of boys work in a field beside the campus.

He also found a "very crooked, ugly gully which ran almost every direction before it got across" the property. Using "the school's boys, the three mules and horse," they cut a ditch eight feet wide and 300 feet long to take its place, and filled in the gully. He was satisfied that the farm "will be very much improved in appearance and in much better shape for cultivating." If that weren't enough to help the boys sleep at night, they also lent a hand in stringing "about 1000 yards of barbed wire fence."

There was one little bit of fun on the farm, however. "We also dug a potato cellar under the new part of the barn, and as we struck a large rock, we had to do a good deal of blasting," Taul recalled. "The boys enjoyed this very much, so much that they wanted to blast all the rocks in sight."[4]

Superintendent Weakley, who came on board the same year, also lamented on the condition of the farm. "There is much to do before we can get our farm in a high state of cultivation, for the land is almost entirely worn out, and it will necessarily take several years of hard work to place it on a paying basis." He reported "about twenty boys regularly working on the farm, who receive instruction in agriculture the same as the other children receive lessons in the shops. They work half of the day and spend the remaining part in school."[5]

The farm had a good yield that year, with 450 bushels of sweet potatoes—the "finest in the valley," according to Weakley—plus 300 bushels of corn, 100 bushels of Irish potatoes, 75 gallons of sorghum syrup, and ample quantities of vegetables and peanuts.[6] They produced hay for their stock and supplemented it with the excess roughage from their corn crop. Taul estimated the total value of what was produced that year on the farm to be approximately $660.[7]

Taul also gave a positive report on his farmhands. "I will say in conclusion that the farm boys have done remarkably well, and have been as easily controlled as the ordinary farm labor, and if they have good tools and stock to work with, they will take pride and pleasure in working on the farm. The greatest drawback now is the lack of land and stock to give all the boys employment who want to work on the farm."[8]

In summarizing his first year, Weakley weighed in on the intrinsic value of farming. "Realizing the free and independent life of an industrious farmer, the good he can accomplish and his position as an honorable citizen, we do all in our power to encourage the children to take up this line of work as their life study."9

The dairy operation was also upgraded during Weakley's first year at the school. Six cows, mostly Jerseys and Guernseys, were purchased, and as funds allowed, the dairy was modernized to include sterilizers, refrigerators, a pasteurizer, and a bottling machine. They were soon producing enough milk for one quart a day per boy.10

In one annual report, Weakley gave special accolades to a cow named Old Blue. Her production over two years was nearly 14,779 pounds of milk valued at over $1139.90. It seems odd to hear milk measured by the pound, but that was and still is the unit of measurement used in the dairy business. After subtracting the cost of Old Blue's feed, she had made the school $867.53.

In the same report, Weakley mentioned the keen interest that the boys had taken in their respective cows and their production, along with the following comment: "The boys claim the cows as their own, give them affectionate names, and are quite jealous of each others' cows."11

Weakley told a story in his papers that demonstrates the boys' attachment to their cows. Two boys were milking their cows side-by-side, when one of the fellows kicked the other boy's cow. As Weakley put it, this was "an overt act no self-respecting dairyman would ever tolerate." The custodian of the unsuspecting cow grabbed the other boy by the collar and angrily threatened, "Look here, boy! If you ever kick my cow again, I'll knock you loose from your inferiority complex." That's probably not the therapy that Freud had in mind for that disorder, but under the circumstances, it most likely eliminated the problem.12

One of Colonel Weakley's favorite stories concerned the time he sent one of the boys to find and return the dairy farm's bull, Old Jerry, who had broken out of the pasture. Weakley waited and waited, but neither the boy nor Old Jerry returned. Years later, Weakley received the following letter:

Dear Colonel Weakley,
  Twenty years ago, you sent me to look for Old Jerry. I have been in

every State in the Union looking for him, and now I am down here in Mexico still looking, and if I find him I will bring him back."

As time went on, there was literally a passing from the old, primitive ways of the past into the new, modern way of farming. In his 1925 report, Weakley referred to some of this and showed his wit in doing so. "We will need next year a new tractor—the old one has asthma, and just at the most critical time it has a very inconvenient habit of emitting a few wheezy coughs and then goes into a state of coma," he wrote. "It usually takes about ten hours of a mechanic's time and a barrel of gasoline to resuscitate it."[13]

On a more serious note, he told of the passing of a friend. "During the year we lost by death one of our mules, Jim. This faithful animal was at the School when I came here twenty-one years ago. Jim was the only living thing on the place that was here when I came, and while it is not my intention to pay a lengthy tribute to his memory, I think it proper to mention him in passing. He served us well throughout his useful life, and in his going we sensed a personal loss. As it often happens with human life, after he was too old for active service, we turned him out to graze in idleness on the best and greenest pastures—in fact we pensioned him."[14]

The size and production of the farm continued to grow. In 1931, farm manager Joe Walden gave a detailed account on every conceivable crop from green beans to field peas to English peas; from turnip greens to collards to cabbage to lettuce; not forgetting Irish potatoes and sweet potatoes, or the abundance of onions, radishes, tomatoes, and carrots. The biggest seller was tomatoes, which generated a profit of nearly $1,200, but the lettuce netted less than $50. The total profit on the crops was $10, 418.83.

As for the dairy, the herd now consisted of twenty-nine cows, fifteen calves, and two bulls. Nearly 235,000 pounds of milk was produced at a value of $11,725.70.[15]

In 1945, just a few years before Weakley's retirement, a *Birmingham News* article provided a good rundown of the farm. "The school operates a 230-acre farm and practical instruction is given in farming, gardening, care of stock and farm machinery operation. About 75 acres are planted in hay, corn, oats, and other field crops; 23 acres in vegetables and about 46 acres are used for pastures. Farm equipment includes a tractor and plow, mower, disc harrow and other smaller tools. The farm has five mules, about 65 hogs and pigs and about 67 cows, heifers, calves and mules."[16]

As for keeping the boys on the farm, Weakley addressed the attitude of the farm squad in one of his reports, stating, "As a whole, we find the farm boys are more willing to work than the others, and I must say they deserve great credit for the manner in which they perform their duties."

In his report, Walden may have revealed the secret. "The boys have been better satisfied and seemed to take more interest in their work this year than usual; one reason for this, I think, has been the picnics and outings that we have enjoyed this summer."[17]

Professor Hart could have learned a thing or two from the shrewd staff at the Alabama Boys' Industrial School. He just did not know that a simple picnic every now and then could help fight the allure of those big city lights.

13

Training Heart, Head, and Hands

Most schools of the early 1900s emphasized a heavy dose of readin', 'ritin', and 'rithmetic. The schoolmasters at the Alabama Boys' Industrial School found that a fourth "R" of rehabilitation was also necessary as the boys' academic perspective and performance needed some serious attention.

Superintendent C. D. Griffin discovered the enormity of his task soon after beginning work at the institution. With some of the students, the teachers were literally starting from scratch. "Their advance in their studies

Students pose for a picture during study hall.

is remarkable," he wrote in the second biennial report. "Some boys who were not able to make their letters or spell a word when received at the school can in six months write a creditable letter. Some of them soon become experts in figures. The boys show a rapid mental alertness as soon as the effects of tobacco, cigarettes and other bad habits are eradicated."[1]

No one doubts the deplorable conditions with which Griffin had to contend. The boys were ill-prepared for academic life, and the resources he was given were totally lacking. Any progress the boys might have made given the situation at hand was admirable. Nevertheless, David Weakley found much to do when he was hired in 1905.

"There was no graded school system; the boys just picked out books they thought they would enjoy," he recalled in his private papers. "Our school was equipped with about forty good desks. Otherwise, there was nothing to inspire the boys for a desire for learning. After tests, both written and oral, we found the boys ranged in grades from first through tenth. A few of the boys had never attended school. During the first few months, we all were engaged in teaching periods, and sometimes, because we were so busy during the day, we would hold night classes."[2]

Statistics for 1906 give some indication of the scope of the problem by detailing the situations from which the students had come. In that year, based on 111 total students, seventy-four had run away from home; ninety-three had been truant at one time or another, sixty-one were neither in school or working at the time of entry. Only thirteen students were regularly attending school at the time of admission.[3]

As the Weakleys became organized, the academic program began to take shape. Mrs. Weakley, who held a degree in education and languages from Peabody College, took charge of the task until a principal and teachers could be hired.

"The boys, as a whole, were eager to learn, and I don't think we ever had a finer bunch of boys than the ones who were at the school when we came," he remembered. "There were, of course, a few who were mentally retarded and were not capable of advancing very far, but we did give them our special attention, and some of them did learn to read and write.

"We felt we were making real progress. The boys in high school were average or above, and their advancement was amazing. Some rated superior. They had been starving at the gates of plenty, and they seemed to recognize this was their golden opportunity."[4]

In the first of Weakley's annual reports, this progress and his future plans were made clear. "The active school hours are divided into four periods of about two hours each. Half of the pupils attend school in the forenoon and the remainder in the afternoon; this arrangement enables us to run both the shops and the school the entire day.

"It is our aim to make the school department second to none in the State, regardless of location or position," he wrote.[5]

In the 1905 report, the academic unit provided a listing of the subjects taught, along with the textbook or materials used. The first, second, and third grades consisted of reading, writing, spelling, and arithmetic. Geography was added to the fourth-grade curriculum, and English history was added to the mix in grades five and six. Grade seven picked up the pace with civil government, algebra and Latin, while grade eight included physics. Some of those 93 truants were probably shaking their heads and wondering what hit them.[6]

One challenge that the school continually had to wrestle was the educational level of the boys when they arrived on campus. A report in 1931 clearly described the scope of the problem. According to the report, "there was not a pupil in the first grade of normal age. The youngest boy 9 and the oldest 16. Second grade boys' ages vary from 9 to 17. Junior third pupils' ages range from 11 to 17." Out of approximately 524 students enrolled that year, only 45 were functioning at an age-appropriate grade.[7]

That does not mean that the students sent to ABIS were lacking in ability. One report made quite clear the reason for this disconnect between grades and ages. "We find a fairly good interest manifested by the pupils of this institution. Of course, there are some who do not seem to take much interest in books, but the most of our boys are bright, industrious, and intelligent, and take advantage of every opportunity offered them."[8] The following year, Weakley went even further in his assessment as he proclaimed, "The children in the school have as a rule made excellent records in their books, the greatest number of them being promoted during our annual examinations. Some have made two grades in one year."[9]

So, the boys needed a caring, competent staff of teachers to help them succeed. One asset the school always had was teachers who seemed to understand the true worth of education and who were eager to instill these values in the boys they instructed. Weakley was always quick to give his faculty the credit they deserved, such as this comment in a yearly report: "Too much praise cannot be given the teachers for the noble manner in which they have labored in the school room and in their other duties in order that they might aid humanity."[10]

In the academic report for 1905, two teachers, Mr. Green and Miss Stamps, wrote of the aspirations they had for their students, and in doing so reveal the character of which Weakley spoke:

> Our aim is to train our pupils to think—to think logically and correctly, for we know that: 'Man's real worth lies in his mind not in his purse.' We try to impress upon them the fact that there is a difference between existing and living. Our course of study is arranged to give the pupil a practical education that will enable him to meet and solve the problems of life, make a useful member of society and a good citizen.
>
> We realize that it is necessary to train the heart, head and hand together. The boy or man with strong intellect and having a strong healthy body but without the moral force necessary to control his feelings and impulses may not only prove himself worthless, but a hindrance and disadvantage to those with whom he comes in contact. Then we should develop all the faculties proportionately.[11]

Longtime principal J. H. Carr echoed those thoughts in his 1908 report:

> Since education is not merely a cold intellectual development but a cultivating of the will, a training of the heart, and building up of durable character, since every human being is a child of God created to do a definite work in the world, we believe that he has a right to a chance in life and ought to be rightly trained to accomplish the work for which God made him. Hence, do we realize the responsibility to instruct the pupil rightly,

and to arouse an enthusiasm in his studies and an ambition in him to become a citizen of whom his county would be proud.[12]

In Weakley's latter years, he proudly told listeners of the fine men the school had produced. Among its graduates were numbered PhDs, physicians, attorneys, military officers, and engineers. There were also musicians, artists, lawmen, and thousands of craftsmen.[13]

Weakley knew that these results were the product of a unique faculty. "Throughout the years, it has been the good fortune of the school to keep in their employ many teachers and instructors whose sole purpose was to contribute something really worthwhile to the sum total of human good and human happiness. Naturally, they have been underpaid, but this does not seem to bother them. They have earned the respect and love of their pupils and the approval of their own conscience."[14]

One of Weakley's favorite stories seems to bring it all together nicely. He frequently told of a Navy officer who returned to his alma mater as a hero of the Pacific theater to tell the ABIS students of his experiences. As he addressed a group of 250 students on the shady lawn, he spotted a white-haired lady slowly making her way down the sidewalk. "There's my old teacher," he exclaimed. With the boys watching, he ran from the stage and threw his arms around the elderly lady. As the two embraced and the sun glinted off his medals, no further explanation was required on what the young officer thought about his education at the Alabama Boys' Industrial School.[15]

14

Present Arms!

If one of today's juvenile reform schools supplied their inmates with Army rifles, the public outcry would be deafening. But the students at the Alabama Boys' Industrial School proved the wisdom of that decision over and over again.

The idea of adding a military component to the school was mentioned by the superintendent in the Second Biennial Report covering 1901–02. "We have not overlooked the military training of our boys," wrote C. D. Griffin. "Regular drills are given them every week and they can march and go through all the military evolutions of a battalion as well as the manual of arms." A photo contained in an early souvenir booklet from the school

This photograph from an early souvenir booklet shows the first group of boys at the school standing at attention. Over the years, a precise military regimen would emerge from this feeble beginning.

Two young cadets appear in dress uniform. Armaments were often furnished through special congressional appropriations, and uniforms were made in the shops on campus.

shows these feeble beginnings with a dozen little boys in knee pants and suspenders giving a feeble salute.[1]

Mrs. Johnston took the concept a step further in her report to the governor for 1905. "The officers and local Board strongly advocate military discipline for the institution," she proposed. "This feature is embodied in the most advanced reform institutions. To be under military restraint and punished by court-martial does not seem to humiliate a boy as do some other modes of correction. Far be it from me to advocate the abolition of the rod, but I do endorse the old divine who said, 'we should pray three times before we whip once.'

"We earnestly desire the cooperation of your Honor in introducing the military system into our work," she continued. "This with uniforms would do much to increase esprit de corps of our institution, without which our school cannot succeed."[2]

The undertaking continued to grow during David Weakley's first year on the job. "We trust in time to be able to secure at least seventy-five rifles, and form a military company . . ." the superintendent wrote in his first report. He further stated that such a concept would be "not only a valuable adjunct to our mode of discipline, but increase in the bosom of the boy a feeling of patriotism and love for his country."[3]

In his personal papers, Weakley elaborated on that point. "We never tried to make our military training tough, but tried to impress upon the pupils the value of discipline and obedience. We felt in all our dealings with the boys, example and precept were more contagious than threats and punishment. Friendship, justice, devotion to duty, with examples of disciplined living, are forces that help turn back the tide of mediocrity and slovenly existence."[4]

From that meager beginning, the program grew in both size and scope. U.S. Senator Oscar Underwood guided a bill through Congress that provided the school with seventy-five military issue rifles. Over the years, several state leaders, including Governor Chauncey Sparks, furnished the school with uniforms and other equipment.[5]

The entire school was soon organized along a military structure, with as many as five or more companies. The boys began to participate in certain ceremonial exercises to start each day, along with having drill two to three times a week for about an hour and a half each session. The Alabama National Guard designated Weakley a colonel as the highest ranking official in the institution. The head of the Military Department was given the rank of lieutenant colonel, and was often a seasoned veteran of some branch of the armed forces.

Weakley described in one of his annual reports the process of mustering in a new cadet. "The new boy is placed in a platoon known as the New Boy Platoon. There he is given instruction without arms, such as position of attention, parade rest, rest, at ease, facing, eyes right or left, hand salute, side step, back step, mark time, quick time, etc. Then he is given a rifle and instruction in the manual of arms before he drills with his company. This takes up a great deal of time and is one of the difficulties of the military instruction for the new boys . . . Here we attempt to tattoo discipline on the boys' minds."⁶

In one of his departmental reports, Lieutenant Colonel H. C. Wood described the total development of the boy as he goes through this demand-

The boys prepare for drill. The officers, with swords, are members of the ABIS staff.

The boys set up camp at Roebuck Springs.

ing routine. "It trains the raw material into a well-ordered being, into the young man ready for the duties and responsibilities of the future," he wrote. "The untrained young man is woefully handicapped in his struggle.

"Military training teaches the young boy how to stand and walk and hold himself erect," he continued. "It gives him vigorous outdoor exercise so that gradually his chest expands and his muscles grow firm. It disciplines him, it develops self control as well as obedience to proper authority, and it prepares the youth for better citizenship."[7]

As the program gained traction, it attempted new and greater challenges. The school started holding drills on Sunday afternoons, which the public was invited to attend. In 1925, this was expanded to an Annual Military Day, with many of the boys being recognized for their achievement. Prizes and medals were given for best-drilled company, best cadet officer, best-drilled cadet, and best all-around boy in the school as determined by the students. Essay contests were held with the boys writing on topics pertaining to citizenship, patriotism, and the like. The commanding officers of the Alabama National Guard and the governor were often in attendance. Weakley estimated that on occasion as many as 4,000 spectators attended from the community.

"I think these public exhibitions gave the boys a feeling of being a part of something worthwhile, and created in them a feeling of self-respect," Weakley commented. "In addition to all this, it gave the public a chance to participate, and to come into our school face to face with the student body, and see first-hand the operation of the school."[8]

One of the most endearing stories from the school's history occurred during one of these ceremonies. According to Weakley, a dog appeared on campus one day, and the boys in one company asked if they could adopt him as their mascot. The colonel gave his permission. Soon the boys had trained their dog to march with them and obey all commands. They even used the school's sewing shop to make the mutt a uniform complete with insignia that identified him as a corporal.

Soon, all the companies had somehow acquired dogs for their squads, and each began trying to outdo the next in the ranks of their four-legged recruits, with none lower than sergeant major. This reached the breaking point one day during the Annual Military Day. The companies filed by the reviewing stand full of local dignitaries and officers from the Alabama National Guard. In perfect step, there appeared a unit led by its mascot proudly wearing a jacket displaying the two stars of a major general! The reviewing officer that day from the National Guard happened to be only a one-star brigadier general. "General," said his aide, as he suppressed a smile, "I see you are outranked today." The obviously embarrassed Weakley busted all dogs back to the rank of private from that day forward.[9]

Another exercise of the school's Military Department took the skills of the cadets to another level. "For several years we had our own military encampment and the U.S. Army regulations prevailed," Weakley wrote in his papers. "The boys lived in tents, did regular guard duty, went through the regular drills, with time provided for tactical study and recreation.

"This was, perhaps, the only time where a school of our type permitted the entire student body to leave the campus for such a purpose," Weakly surmised. "It was a Herculean task, for provision had to be made for cooking, lighting, sleeping, health sanitation, etc. The training proved invaluable to those who entered into World War I."

War, unfortunately, became a reality for many of the boys. According to Weakley, more than 700 ABIS alumni fought in World War I and close to 800 in World War II.[10] Each time one of those young men answered the call to serve, he showed the enormous value that military training had on his own life and for his country.

15

Blowing a Horn

A quotation that some attribute to the famed bandmaster John Philip Sousa goes something like this: "Teach a boy to blow a horn and he will never blow a safe."[1]

The founders of the Alabama Boys' Industrial School certainly agreed with that principle. From the beginning of the institution, the creation of a concert and marching band was on the agenda. Over the next fifty years, this tousle-haired, rag-tag assortment of boys would become one of the finest bands of its kind in the country, to make even Sousa proud.

The notion of a musical band in a correctional facility seems out of place today, but the innovative warden Zebulon Brockway had implemented this rehabilitative concept at New York's Elmira Reformatory in 1876.[2] It is not known where the ABIS leadership got the idea, but C. D. Griffin, the first superintendent, referred to such a plan in the institution's third annual report in 1903.

"One of the most attractive and most useful departments in an institution like ours is the Band," Griffin stated. "It keeps the boys interested, teaches them to read music and may be made a source of profit as well as pleasure when they leave us and strike out for themselves. There is always a chance for a good musician to make money enough for expenses in a new place while looking for something in a band or orchestra."

Dealing with the bleak situation of keeping the new school afloat, Griffin obviously found it difficult to fund a nonessential activity like a band in the midst of more pressing needs. So, his wife came up with a novel idea. "We have a wild plum orchard that yields us an abundant supply of plums annually. Mrs. Griffin devised a scheme whereby a Band Fund could be started by making our surplus plums into jelly for sale," Griffin wrote. "It seemed a good idea and the ladies of the Board thought the product

The band finds a shady place on campus to practice.

could be disposed of to advantage, so the fruit was picked by the boys and worked up into jelly at night after the boys had retired. There were about 800 glasses made, the ladies of the Board selling what they could at $2.50 per dozen glasses."

Apparently plum jelly was not in high demand that season, for the results of that effort are never mentioned. However, one of the school's supporters, a Mr. F. M. Jackson, took up the cause and raised $218 for the band. Mr. Griffin was then able to purchase twenty-two used instruments for $200 [$5,263 in 2013 dollars], a fact that greatly pleased both him and the boys. "Our boys are already enjoying in imagination the fine music we are to have some months in the future when they have learned to use their instruments," Griffin reported. His tenure with the school lasted only an additional year, so he was not on hand to see these musings turn into music.[3]

Griffin's successor, Weakley, was an ardent supporter of the band. When he took the helm in 1905, he immediately took action to move the project forward. His was no easy task, either. Not only did he battle financial realities, but he met with resistance from those who opposed such a program in a school for delinquent boys. "To my surprise, I experienced much opposition from some of the public school teachers," Weakley wrote in his papers some years later. "One Superintendent of Public Schools was outspoken in opposition. In fact he was so antagonistic that I feared for awhile that public opinion would be so wrought-up that I would have to abandon the project." This opponent went on to say that such an enterprise would be "corrupting and disrupting to the whole educational system; that the boys should be taught to work and should not be exposed to such falderal."[4]

Weakley was quite eloquent in his defense of music. The purpose of musical instruction was "not to turn out professional musicians, but to develop an inner response in the heart and minds of our boys to the finer, higher things of life. I believe," Weakley continued, "in the spiritual, mental, and moral exaltation it creates, and the nobility of its influence in correcting and improving human behavior, especially in the lives of the young. It seems to me, that music is a potent force in helping to curb and, perhaps, cure crime." Weakley went on to quote great thinkers who lauded the healing powers of music. Plato, he said, praised "the rhythm and harmony [that] find their way into the inward places of the soul . . ." Shakespeare wrote that "the man who hath not music in his soul . . . is fit for tragedies, treasons, and spoils."[5]

Weakley's arguments eventually convinced the local school official and everyone else, for the band became a reality within a year of his arrival. Some reports indicate that ABIS was the first school of any kind in Alabama to have a band.[6] Initially the band started with fifteen students with Weakley, who had played in bands himself in his youth, as the instructor.[7]

Soon thereafter, John D. Henderson was employed as the school's bandmaster, but he also had to serve as the school's shorthand and typewriting instructor. In his initial report as bandmaster, Henderson wrote of the accomplishments and challenges of working with the new band. He also gave a not-so-subtle commentary on Griffin's purchase of those first instruments off the clearance rack. "I regret to say that our original twenty-two instruments were bought by an inexperienced man, and while the intentions were good,

A couple of band members look very serious about their music.

they could not be considered a bargain at any price, as their musical qualities, and not their weight in brass, should have been taken into consideration." The fine musician was not deterred, however, for within six weeks the band was already playing some simple compositions.[8]

Colonel Weakley was not the only one to extol the benefits of the band for the students and the school. In her portion of the report, Mrs. Johnston noted that "a boy failing in good conduct is suspended from the band, making this not only a source of pleasure, but also a means of discipline."[9] Henderson commented that all schools need a "time for recreation, both physically and mentally." He also wrote of its "educational and pecuniary advantages" and of its "effective method of bringing the School and its work before the public . . ."[10]

So, go before the public they did. Their skills developed to such a level in their first year that they were selected to lead the parade when President Theodore Roosevelt paid a visit to Birmingham. Later that day they paraded by the president's reviewing stand decked out in Rough Rider uniforms in his honor. When someone whispered to him "There come Mrs. Johnston's boys," the president clapped his hands and shouted his trademark "Bully, Bully!"[11]

If it is possible to go any higher than performing for the president of the United States, this group did it over the next forty years. After several years, Henderson left to assume another position and was replaced by Eugene Jordan. Under Jordan's twenty-five year tutelage, the band's fame spread throughout the nation.[12] Over the years, the band made several appearances in Washington, D.C. They gave a performance in front of the Capitol, and also accompanied the U.S. Marine Band in concert in one of the city's parks.[13] In 1922, the band went on an extended six-week trip on the Keith Vaudeville Circuit through Tennessee, Arkansas, and Texas.[14]

The band, averaging sixty members, was a "must" at any event and parade in Alabama. The 1931 Annual Report shows the band made fifty-four appearances that year alone, ranging from the Howard College vs. Birmingham-Southern football game to the Ruhama Baptist Church service to a Lions Club luncheon. They made a broadcast on WAPI radio, played at the season-opening baseball game at Rickwood Field, serenaded the

This publicity photograph shows the band during one of John Philip Sousa's appearances in Birmingham. The adults in front are, from left to right, Mrs. Johnston, Sousa, and ABIS band director E. C. Jordan. Captain Jordan's picture is also shown in the inset at the top. The photo was taken during World War I when Sousa served as a lieutenant commander and led the Naval Reserve Band in Illinois.

First Methodist Church, and gave a concert at the Old Soldiers Reunion in Montgomery. They played for the Ice Cream Manufacturer's Convention at the Tutwiler Hotel, in the Better Business Bureau parade, and at a function for the LeHigh Cement Company in Tarrant City.[15]

With as many trips and engagements as these boys had, a few memorable occurrences were bound to happen. One such incident happened during an engagement in a neighboring city. Jordan was leading the band down the street when he was approached by a small boy.

"Say, mister, how can you get in this band?" he asked.

"You shouldn't worry about getting into this band," Jordan simply replied.

A few blocks later the boy appeared again and said, "I want in this band. How can I get in?"

"Run along, son. You see I am busy," Jordan gently told him. However the boy persisted and asked again.

"Just break out some windows," the bandmaster said jokingly just to get rid of the tyke.

A few months later back at the school, a youngster met Jordan on the sidewalk. The boy saluted and said, "Well, here I am."

"Who are you?" asked Jordan.

"I'm the boy you told to break out some windows," the new student answered.

"Oh, son, you didn't really do that, did you?" Jordan sighed.

"Yes, sir, I did, and I like to never have made it. Some of those welfare ladies would beg and ask for another chance. I finally had to break a plate glass window before I made it," he proclaimed proudly.

Since he had merely taken Professor Jordan's advice, they just had to let him in the band.[16]

Colonel Weakley once had the opportunity to provide some needed guidance to one of the band members. The student's school work had declined, and the colonel stopped by to see about the problem. "Colonel, I'll be plain with you," the boy finally confessed. "I'm in love." He then explained that while the band had been on a recent trip to Anniston, he had fallen for a young girl with whose family he had stayed on the overnight trip.

"Well, I've never known it to kill a man, son," Weakley advised. "But if you've really got it bad, maybe you'd better learn to make enough money to afford a wife." The young man did just that by learning to be a typesetter. Two years later, the couple married and moved to North Carolina, where he took a job with a newspaper.[17]

The band had one other case of puppy love. Weakley recalled in his papers a collie named Corporal that came to live at the school. He became every boy's pet, and was therefore terribly spoiled. Corporal was especially fond of the band, went to their practices, and followed them when they rehearsed their marching.

One day the band was giving a performance a few miles down the road in East Lake. In the middle of one of the numbers, Corporal came bounding down the center aisle and tried to jump on the stage with the band. The stage was so high that only his front legs reached the platform, leaving the remainder of the concert-loving canine dangling in the air, howling along with the music. Without missing a beat, the director leaned down and pulled Corporal up, where he stood at attention for the remainder of the show.[18]

Through the years, the ABIS Band received plaudits from the Kiwanis and Rotary clubs, commendations from several chambers of commerce, and favorable comments from editorials in the *Montgomery Advertiser* and the *Birmingham News*, to name a few.[19]

Perhaps their biggest fan was the man whose stirring marches they could play by heart, John Philip Sousa. The great bandmaster and composer came to Birmingham for a performance, and the boys were a part of the welcoming party.[20] The famed maestro directed the band during the intermission of his concert, and presented them with his prestigious Loving Cup.[21] At the conclusion, he shook hands with the boys, posed for pictures and complimented them as possibly the finest boys' band he had ever heard.[22]

Undoubtedly Sousa also recognized that as well as these boys could blow a horn, the safes around Birmingham were in no danger.

A cover from one of the early editions of The Boys' Banner, *which was written and printed by ABIS students for three quarters of a century.*

16

THE BOYS' BANNER

In April of 1901, C. D. Griffin wrote in his diary the following simple statement: "John printed the cover to our first paper, and I think he has made a first class job of it." The following month, he added that John had also "paid 50 cents subscription for the Banner. He is our first subscriber."[1] So, with little fanfare, *The Boys' Banner*, the student-run periodical of the Alabama Boys' Industrial School, was born.

The publication, full of news items, campus gossip, inspiring feature stories, jokes, and even poetry, endured for three-quarters of a century. Published on campus by the students in the print shop, the *Banner* was sometimes in newspaper format and at other times in magazine format. Depending upon the situation and the times, it was available on a monthly or even weekly basis. Articles were written by the students or were reprints from other publications of the day.

Below are representative samples of the material found in the *Boys' Banner*, such as this excerpt from a news account from 1924:

BOYS ENJOY VITAGRAPH FEATURE
    Saturday, March 8, thru the kindness of Mr. T. G. Coleman, manager of the Galax Theatre, Birmingham, the boys of this school were offered a real pleasure in having presented to them "Pioneer Trails," a first-run Vitagraph moving picture, which certainly was enjoyed by the boys, who wish to thank Mr. Coleman and the Vitagraph Company for letting the picture be shown out here before its presentation in Birmingham.[2]

An October 1924 entry announced an event of a more spiritual nature:

BIBLE CLASS
   The Bible Class has just recently been organized, two months ago.
   We wish to thank Mr. Sutton for giving us the nice new Bibles, which he bought for our class. We are trying to do what he tells us to do. We are learning the books of the Old Testament which we are studying hard to learn.
   There are twelve boys in the Bible Class. Mr. Sutton comes out here every Thursday night as it is meeting night, and we go to the chapel and recite our lessons that Mr. Sutton has given us to learn for the next meeting night.[3]

The *Banner* also did its best to keep up with the social scene as it applied to the faculty and staff.

FRAZIER, LYONS WEDDING EVENT OF AUGUST
   A wedding of interest was that of Miss Virginia Frazier, second daughter of Mrs. Pearl Arrington Frazier, Tallassee, Ala. and Mr. George Lyons, only son of Mr. and Mrs. A. E. Lyons which was solemnized at the First Baptist Church.
   The ceremony which witnessed by friends was performed by Dr. L. O. Dawson.
   The bride is a graduate of the Tallassee High School and has been attending Florence Normal and has been on the teaching staff here for several years. Mr. Lyons has been serving as officer at this institution for some time.[4]

Sports articles made up a significant part of the periodical. This 1936 article heralded the beginning of football practice, and also showcased the style of the sportswriter.

AMATEURS BEGIN PRACTICE ON THE GRID
   The season for the great Autumn sport football has opened with 40 tryouts sprinting across the cow pasture clad in shorts and shoes, working off some of their superfluous flesh. These young enthusiasts welcome the

opportunity of giving the old pigskin a few forceful plasters.

Very rigid rules are adhered to for success in this game. It is necessary to leave off all harmful drugs, tea, coffee, spirits, tobaccos, and late hours if you expect to be one of a winning team. Instances in big teams where members have been expelled simply for eating pies in disobedience to rules.

Coach Nunnally and Ball have found a football field for practicing. It is a cow pasture, way back in the sticks.[5]

An article from 1932 detailed an important event attended by the school's team:

FOOTBALL TEAM SEES IMPORTANT GAME AT LEGION FIELD
Last Saturday, November the nineteenth, the A.B.I.S football team went to Legion Field and enjoyed a football game between Howard[*] and Birmingham Southern Colleges. The game was very close and interesting, but Southern finally won seven to nothing. Most of the boys wanted Howard to win, because some of our school teachers are from Howard, and Mr. Bob Shelton, head football coach at the school, is an ex-football player and student at Howard College. Mr. Owen Williams, athletic director of the school is also a Howard student. All of the football boys have been seeing these football games through the courtesy and kindness of Mr. Shelton and Mr. Williams, who have been securing the transportation and passes for the games.[6]

Another sports account trumpeted the success of the season-ending football banquet.

HARRY GILMER AND VIRGIL TRUCKS ATTEND BIG FOOTBALL BANQUET
With such outstanding sports personalities as Harry Gilmer and Virgil Trucks present, the school's 1945 Football Banquet—voted the best in A.B.I.S. history—was held last Friday evening in the Boys Dining Hall.

---

[*] Howard is now Samford University. Due to its location in the East Lake community, the college had a close relationship with ABIS during its formative years. In 1957, Samford moved to a new campus in Homewood.

Gilmer, Alabama's All-American, was a surprise guest. He spoke briefly and also visited boys who were unable to attend the festivities. Virgil Trucks, Detroit Tiger World Series pitching hero, also spoke.[7]

In most editions, news from the various campus units was included, such as:

FARM REPORT
The farm boys have been very busy for the past month getting ready for the winter by gathering the corn and the various things that we raised this year.

Mr. Joe Walden has charge of the farm and all the boys like him just fine.

We are at the present hauling coal for the boiler room, we are using two two-horse wagons and four mules also one mare which proves a great help to us.

There are twenty-two boys on the farm force, all of them are healthy and like the farm just fine. We will soon be able to go hunting when we get through with our work.[8]

An announcement from the Academic Department boasted of some new equipment:

MICROSCOPE STUDY NOW USED IN CLASSES
Full equipment for microscopic study in connection with science and biology classes may soon be acquired by the A.B.I.S. school it was learned today. Boys in 10th and 11th grades are using a microscope to study plant and animal cells, etc.[9]

Some of the departmental reports contained a little subtle editorializing along with the facts:

LAUNDRY
We are getting along fine in the laundry now. Mr. T. W. Branham is our instructor.

We are doing a lot of work, but we have to keep busy to keep caught up.

We have a large crew of boys working in the laundry. Henry _____, who is better known as "Squashy," is our best check boy. He is so lazy Mr. Branham has to tell him to keep off the baskets and sit on a stool, for he will fall over in a laundry basket and go to sleep.

We washed the following number of articles the past month: 5804 towels, 1189 unionalls, 978 table cloths, 2101 pair socks, 620 napkins, 1208 sheets, 1189 suits of underwear, besides work for the officers and teachers.[10]

This entry from 1934 also engaged in some good-natured ribbing:

BOYS IN BARBER SHOP HAVE NO TIME TO LOAF

This shop under the supervision of Mr. Lingo sure can transform the long-haired grizzly faced ugly duckling to the young swans of our school. They have a long mirror on the wall that give the boy a chance to view himself before and after. The gallants come out with their hair sleeked back and combed, thus becoming our Beau Brummels.[11]

Much of the campus news and gossip was relayed to the readers with simple, often pithy one-liners, such as the following:

Billie _____ underwent a very serious operation at Hillman Hospital recently. He seems to be improving, and we wish him a speedy recovery.[12]

Mr. Seale has been replacing window panes which got broken during the snow battles last week. He also has repaired the porch of the Johnston Building.[13]

A certain Professor is sort of hiding the fact that last Saturday he flushed eight covey of birds and in company with the other Nimrods knocked down exactly six birds. Mr. Baker says that's something of a record of the wrong kind.[14]

What do you think of a fellow who was so anxious to get a letter from his girl that he rang up the postmaster at night and asked if a letter came for him in the last mail?[15]

If Doyle _____, right fielder for the senior team, could keep from getting hung up in the fences, maybe we could beat Acipco.[16]

One of the features for which *The Boys' Banner* became known was articles reprinted from other publications which tried to instill virtue in the students.

IT'S THE MAN WHO DOES THINGS

It is not the critic who counts; not the man who points out how the strong man stumbled or where the do'er of deeds could have done them better. The credit belongs to the man who is actually in the arena; whose face is marred by dust and sweat and blood; who strives valiantly; who errs and comes short again and again, because there is no effort without error and shortcomings; who does actually strive to do the deed; who knows the great enthusiasm, the great devotions, spends himself in a worthy cause; who at the best knows in the end the triumph of high achievement; and at the worst, if he fails, he at least fails while daring greatly, so that his place shall never be with those cold and timid souls who know neither victory nor defeat.—Theodore Roosevelt[17]

This piece of advice from a 1907 issue would still be appropriate today:

DON'T SMOKE, BOYS

There are plenty of good reasons why boys should not contract the habit of smoking, and various ways of stating them. The editor saw a practical statement of that kind a few days ago and he quotes it for what good it may do in spite of the fact that is not new. A man who had more time than the editor can spare made a calculation showing that three cigars a day, at a cost of 10 cents each, for forty-five years from the age of 20 to 65, would amount, at 6 percent, compounded annually to the snug little fortune of $18,100.14. Save the money, boy, and your health at the same time.[18]

This article seemed particularly relevant for some of the boys who might call ABIS home:

A MISTAKE OFTEN MADE

Boys and young men sometimes start out in life with the idea that one's success depends on sharpness and chicanery. They imagine if one is able always to "get the best of the bargain," no matter by what deceit or meanness he carries his point, that his prosperity is assured. This is a great mistake. Enduring prosperity cannot be founded on cunning and dishonesty. The tricky and deceitful man is sure to fall a victim, soon or late, to the influences which are forever working against him.—The Exchange[19]

This piece of wisdom from 1936 would have been useful for the thieves in residence:

FOR WHAT WE GET WE HAVE TO PAY

Life is a market place, and everything in it costs something—nothing is given free; if it is, it's not worth having. Willingness to pay is the price of success, and money is not the only coinage; we pay with thought, long, hard thoughts; with effort, the long pull of persistent toil, with courage, the moral dynamic force which the spirit supplies, and with sacrifice, the giving up of pleasures that are not necessary.[20]

Even the poetry that was included in most every issue had a lesson, like the first stanza of this poem:

IT MUST BE GREAT

    It must be great to stop and wait
    When heated words are spoken,
    And so create a truce-like state,
    That saves what might be broken,
    When passions arise, they dim the size
    Of grievous altercation,
    And minimize what's most the prize,

A placid reservation. —The Vocational Enterprise[21]

This poem could have been just the remedy for the boy who was downhearted:

JUST AROUND THE CORNER
    When you're feeling kind of "bluish"
    And life does not seem just right
    When the sunshine seems to darken
    And the day turn to night,
    Don't give up and start to worry
    If your ship begins to list
    Maybe just around the corner
    Is the joy you have always missed.

    Then throw back your shoulders,
    March along with head erect;
    Laugh when trouble comes to mock you,
    And your plans seem all but wrecked,
    There is One whose love is mighty,
    Every thought of doubt resist,
    He is waiting, round the corner
    With the things you've always missed. —The Advance[22]

The back page of every issue was filled with jokes, usually headed by catchy titles such as "Rib Crackers," "Shirt-Slitters," "Funnybone Ticklers," and "Grin and Bear It."

    Teacher: If I subtract 80 from 195, what is the difference?
    Young Doubtful: Yeah, that's what I say; who cares?

    New Arrival: Do you know if the charges are reduced if one stays a week?
    Hotel Porter: Could not tell you, sir. Nobody's ever stayed a week.

Corporal: I hear that the drill sergeant called you a blockhead.
Private: No, he didn't make it that strong.
Corporal: What did he actually say?
Private: Put on your hat; here comes a woodpecker.[23]

Angry wife: Are all men fools?
Husband: No, dear, some are bachelors.

Doctor: Well, how are you today?
Patient: I'm better that I was before, but I ain't as good as I was before I got as bad as I am now.[24]

An ABIS baseball player puts on his game face before taking the field.

17

A Winning Reputation

The value of physical education is too well known for me to dwell upon it, but if it is necessary in high school and colleges, I feel that it is more necessary in a school of our type," David Weakley once wrote. "It stimulates competition, creates companionship, develops self-confidence, loyalty, and a feeling of esprit de corps."[1]

Those words provided the foundation for what would become a comprehensive athletic program for the Alabama Boys' Industrial School. Like all schools, its sports teams had their share of ups, downs, and memorable moments.

One of the first recorded accounts of ABIS athletic competition was in 1907, when an article in *The Boys' Banner* reported the school's baseball team defeating The Ensleys six to two in a rain-shortened contest.[2] One of the spectators at the game was none other than Judge Feagin of the local police court, a figure well-known to the hometown team for obvious reasons. *The Banner* mentioned that he "made a short talk to the entire school in which he gave them some excellent advice." One would imagine that the topic of that speech covered more than just balls and strikes.[3]

Another article that same season showed that boys from a century ago were not immune to the trash talking that has become so common among today's athletes. The *Banner* article is printed below just as it appeared, with quotations and unusual spelling intact. Some of the inferences have been lost to time, but the intent to poke fun at their opponents remains clear.

> The B.I.S. ball club is fast becoming a "holy terror" to all aspiring Knights of the Diamond. The visiting teams come "trabbling up de road" with a look in their eyes, as much as to say, "Oh, well, it's hardly worthwhile to fool our time away with these boys at the school, but

ABIS competed against local high schools in a number of sports, including baseball.

they need practice and we will help them out."

They certainly do help the boy to get practice, but not in the way the visitors expect.

The first victims of the deceptive curves of the gentleman from "Cairo" was the Ensleys. After that the gentlemen from the Birmingham post office, who were deluded into the fact that because they could throw letters fifty ways for Sunday in Uncle Sam's letter field, they could put up an equally good showing on the B.I.S. ball grounds.

Next came the "terrors" from East Lake with a record of 21 games won and one lost. Well, it is hardly worthwhile making any comments, as the score table will tell.

The included box score showed that the ABIS boys did back up the big talk of their cocky scribe by defeating East Lake two to nothing.[4]

The loss of some of the *Banner's* issues makes it impossible to accurately trace the emergence of the athletic program. It has not been determined if the teams were in continuance existence or may have been suspended from time to time due to financial difficulties, World War I, and other factors. For whatever reason, athletic activity begins to be mentioned again prominently in the 1930s.

A *Banner* piece from 1932 looked to the start of the basketball season with optimism.

> Coach Williams is going to have charge of the basketball team, and he sure does know his stuff when it comes to playing basketball. The school's prospect for a winning team is very good, with veterans returning from last year's team.[5]

A 1938 *Banner* article also held high hopes for a victorious season, along with some impressive prose from an aspiring sportswriter.

> "Shoot! Hey! Nice shot, Harvey!" Once again these familiar cries re-echo through the gymnasium of the school as the Golden Tornadoes of the Alabama Boys' Industrial School begin their training for the coming basketball season. The crashing of bodies, perspiration, smell of wintergreen; all these remind us that basketball is with us once more and will be king for several months. Now is the time of the year that the Rose Bowl, the World Series and the "champ" are almost forgotten for the thrills and the glamour of the basketball court.[6] (Golden Tornadoes Train, *Boys' Banner*, January, 1938, p. 3)

The nickname Golden Tornadoes is used periodically during this period, but in the following years it was common to hear the teams referred to as the Golden Raiders, as in this report from 1945.

> With a record of two wins, one tie and a loss, the Golden Raiders courtmen journey to Trussville today for a tussle with Hewitt High School.

> Today's game against Hewitt will mark the first time an A.B.I.S court team will invade an opponent's court.[7]

It is interesting to speculate if the rare occurrence of a road game was due to security concerns on the part of ABIS, the reluctance of other schools to host this team from the reform school, or simply due to travel and financial constraints.

Team sports were not the only activities offered at the school. Boxing and track are also mentioned in the annals of the institution, and given the skills involved in these two sports—and the requisite talent some of the residents were known to possess in that regard—it is not surprising that the ABIS boys would be competitive. A 1945 story made this proud announcement:

> Top ranking runners of this institution will be entered in the Southeastern A.A.U. three mile road race on December 8th it was announced today. It will mark the first time A.B.I.S. has competed under A.A.U. auspices.[8]

In a similar vein, the *Banner* touted the prospects of the boxing squad:

> The A.B.I.S. glove slingers have been working hard for the past three months with their eyes on the Golden Gloves tournament to be held at the city auditorium in February. They have been meeting the cream of the crop of fighters around Birmingham and more than holding their own. Indeed their reputation has spread so that sometimes it is hard to match them.
>
> The boxing team was organized last January. At the Golden Gloves tournament, A.B.I.S had four entrants who made a creditable showing although handicapped by lack of experience. To gain this experience, Mr. Ball and Mr. Nunnelley have been matching this year's team in all the local amateur shows held this fall. Out of 21 fights, the boys from A.B.I.S. have won 10, drew 9, and lost only four. Now with the Golden Gloves tournament only a few weeks off, the team is working out each night in the gym. So don't be surprised if we win a couple of state championships.[9]

Despite all of these athletic pursuits, it should come as no surprise in Alabama that football seemed to be the favorite sport of all. More attention—and ink in the *Banner*—was given to this fall mainstay than any other. The football program appears to have started in the 1930s under Coach "Jum" Nunnelley, and that period also was its heyday in terms of victories. A *Banner* article from 1938 summarized the team's recent success.

> Coach Nunnally's football team blocked, tackled, passed and kicked themselves to new and greater glory by emerging victorious another year. One defeat in 16 games, that's the record for the past two seasons which the Boys' Industrial School football team boasts. This season the team won seven and lost but one, while in 1936 it was undefeated and untied in an eight game schedule. Total scores for the campaigns will show the ease with which the industrial lads overcame the majority of their opposition. In '36 the team piled up a total of 245 points to 25 for the opposition; this season they ran up a 190 point total to 19 for opponents.[10]

It did not take long for the school to descend from such dizzying heights. As the grid team fell on hard times, the *Banner*, with tongue in cheek, blamed it on supernatural forces.

> A new member seems to have been playing on the school's football team for the first two games of the season, to judge by the outcome of the two games, and the entire student body is arming itself with stout hickory clubs in an effort to be ready to send this unwanted member, Old Man Jinx, to the unhappy haunted grounds, or some other remote place.[11]

Not only did the record on the field plummet, but the school actually became dependent on outside support to equip its team. *The Birmingham News* printed a letter from Colonel Weakley thanking Marshall Durbin of the City Salesmen's Club for their support.

> Col. D. M. Weakley, superintendent of Boys' Industrial School, in a letter to Durbin expressed hearty approval and appreciation of the plan

to raise funds for the football team. He declared he felt that if the Industrial School boys were properly equipped they could compete on equal footing with other teams. It would instill in them a feeling of confidence and pride, he pointed out.[12]

Even the new uniforms and pads did not help. The 1945 squad fell to rock bottom, winning only one game against eleven losses, including a school record defeat of sixty to nothing at the hands of Cordova High School. It fell to Coach Ray Kruger to come up with some motivation. After going scoreless in the first six games of the season, he offered a "sizzling steak" to the first player to score a touchdown for the Golden Raiders. One of the ABIS defenders intercepted a Bessemer pass and scampered sixty-five yards for a touchdown and a sirloin, but the hard-luck eleven still lost the game eight to seven. Something inspired the entire team, however, for they won their only game the following week 54 to zero with nothing at stake—or steak—but pride.[13]

In addition to several varsity sports, ABIS had recreation for all the students. In this photograph, officers supervise a recreation period.

After such a lousy season, it is only natural to look for small victories. In a wrap-up to this season-to-forget, the *Banner* sportswriter found one bright spot.

> Noteworthy indeed, is the fact that the Raiders were penalized only once for anything other than an offside. In all they received only thirteen penalties, winning for themselves a reputation for being one of the cleanest teams in this area. In this writer's little book, that counts a great deal more than a list of figures in the win column.[14]

In fact, that is quite a remarkable feat for a team of so-called "bad boys." Given Colonel Weakley's stated goals for his athletic program, that is the stuff of which champions are made.

18

AMEN

"Why shouldn't I have faith?" Elizabeth Johnston once asked. "The manifestation of God's help has ever been with the school. Trusting God is one of the most thrilling experiences man can enjoy."[1]

In the grand tradition of Christianity, Mrs. Johnston wanted her boys to have the joy of that same relationship with their Heavenly Father, and saw to it that the school she founded at least gave them that opportunity. After all, it was God who had given her the charge, provided her with the courage to fight the battles, and met her every need time and time again. How could she fail to at least tell her boys his story?

No doubt there was another factor, at least in the minds of some, that made religious instruction altogether appropriate for such an institution. What harm could possibly be done by introducing these so-called bad boys to basic moral and spiritual values that might have a positive impact on their less than desirable behavior? An ample dose of the Bible might be the perfect cure for that affliction as well.

So it was with these two compelling reasons, Sunday School, worship services, and daily devotionals became a staple at the Alabama Boys' Industrial School. It was not uncommon during this era, in fact, for biblical instruction to be found in state-sponsored institutions for youthful offenders all across the nation. In the latter part of the twentieth century, however, these programs came under fire and were largely curtailed due to concerns over the separation between church and state.

In the new millennium, however, religious strategies for dealing with delinquency have reappeared under the mantra of "faith-based programs." The key factors that make these new efforts permissible are the availability of a wide variety of religious faiths in addition to Christianity, and the voluntary—rather than mandatory—nature of the programs.

The Christian faith is still the most prevalent religion found in today's juvenile institutions due to its numerical strength in the American population and the more evangelistic approach of its followers.

Christianity was an ever-present influence from day one at ABIS. In a report from 1902, C.D. Griffin stated, "Different pastors of Birmingham, East Lake and Woodlawn have been very kind to assist us in our Sunday services, and if for some reason a minister fails to keep his appointment, we have the regular service ourselves with a Bible lesson and song service."[2] In his personal papers, Griffin also indicated that Mrs. Johnston herself sometimes taught the Sunday School class for the boys.[3]

When David Weakley assumed the day-to-day management of the school in 1905, Mrs. Johnston could not have found a more supportive ally in her beliefs, as he was also a devout Christian. In expressing his views on the Christian walk in his personal papers, Weakley quoted Maltbie Babcock, a leading theologian of the day: "Christianity is not a voice in the wilderness, but a life in the world. It is not an idea in the air, but feet on the ground going God's way. It is not an exotic to be kept under glass, but a hardy plant to bear twelve months of fruit in all kinds of weather."

Weakley continued by giving some of his own insights. "In a time of stress, when cold reason acknowledges defeat, and we find that philosophy and logic and all our calculated plans and rules have failed, and we are without goals, and fear and failure stalk by our side, and we are adrift in a jungle of doubt; it is then that faith is a waiting door. It is faith in God, faith in prayers, faith in ourselves and faith in the goodness of our fellow man that is a torch that lights the path to truth. Even as it is written, 'Be ye faithful unto death, and I will give you a crown of life.'"

Weakley wrote of the efforts he and his staff made to impart this faith to the students. There were daily Bible readings in each dormitory, as well as during school. Bible classes were conducted each week and chapel services at least twice monthly.[4] "We tried to make our religious services impressive and interesting," he said. "The boys enjoyed singing hymns and discussing in an informal manner the high points of the Sunday School lesson. Our Chapel services, usually held on Sunday afternoons, were conducted by our

Bush Chapel, built with funds donated by original board member Mrs. T. G. Bush.

regular Chaplain. We had our own vested choir with accompaniment by the Hammond organ and our orchestra."[5]

In his annual report for 1915, the head of the academic department, Mr. Carr, provided greater detail on how religious instruction fit within the school's program of study. "In the school, religion occupies a central position. As only one half of the boys attend school in the forenoon and the other half in the afternoon, devotional services are conducted in the study hall twice each day at the opening of the day's work. A selection of scripture is read and such comments are made as will lead the boy to make his own application to life and to bring his heart 'those eternal verities that shall unite humanity and develop a living consciousness of the truth that shall abide forever.' Sectarian spirit and all expressions of denominational prejudice are excluded. 'The great fundamental truths, the existence of God, the immortality of man, man's responsibility, the reality of life beyond death, intimately related to the life we now live,' are among the great truths presented and urged for recognition."[6]

Some of those truths were accepted, as a number of the boys made public professions of their faith each year. Arrangements were then made

The scripture above the entrance of the chapel was specifically selected to speak to the hearts of the boys.

Elizabeth Johnston had a personal relationship with God and wanted nothing less for her boys.

with local ministers for each boy to join the church of his choice in the appropriate manner and generally this would result in a very meaningful service for all of those involved.

On occasion, the boys were asked to put that new faith into action. One day, Mrs. Johnston was teaching a Sunday Bible class when she received a telegram that her grandson was in dire condition and might not survive. She slowly put the telegram in her lap as she regained her composure. "Boys," she said quietly, "this telegram tells me one of my grandsons is not expected to live. Now I want you to put everything aside and silently pray for him." All heads bowed instantly as the boys earnestly prayed for Mrs. Johnston's loved one. A few hours later, another telegram came from Atlanta hailing the miracle that had confounded all of the attending physicians. The boy had rallied and was out of danger. No Bible story could have done as much in teaching the boys the wonder of prayer.[7]

Mrs. Johnston received a letter one day that confirmed the powerful witness she lived before the boys. The letter read, in part, "When you talk to us on Sundays in Chapel, it makes me feel as though I owe something to you. Since you have been talking to us I seem to be a changed boy. I don't feel like I used to, but have a feeling of love for the helpless and poor." Given Mrs. Johnston's own feelings toward the disadvantaged, those words surely touched her heart.[8]

Weakley admitted, however, that some attempts at spirituality were completely lost, as indicated by the following episode.

"There were ten or twelve boys who expressed a desire to unite with the Baptist Church. A Baptist minister came to the School to make the arrangements. At that time we had a swimming pool for the smaller boys about three feet deep and thirty feet in diameter, with an elevated wall eighteen inches high. The pool was surrounded by sycamore and elm trees. It was a restful spot. When the minister saw this pool, he suggested he use it for the baptismal service, stating he thought an outside service, in such a beautiful setting, would be inspirational and impressive. I agreed.

"It was a Sunday afternoon; the sun was slipping to slumber in the West. All was quiet and peaceful. There was a prevalence of reverence and expectation. The minister took one of the boys to the center of the pool and uttered the words, 'I baptize you in the name of the Father, the Son, and the Holy Ghost, amen.' Evidently, he failed to give them the proper instructions, for when he said 'amen,' the boys thought he said 'jump in,' and they did—all in complete unison. They hit the water with a mighty splash, and all I remember is a pyramid of water ascending and cascading over the minister, completely obscuring him from view.

"In retrospect, I would like to know what happened to the first boy immersed, and also what happened to the minister," he concluded. "The story may carry a moral. Frankly, I don't know."[9]

This was obviously not what Mrs. Johnston meant when she said trusting God was a "thrilling experience," but most likely she was amused nonetheless.

19

HEALING BODY AND SOUL

The demands of tending to the medical needs of one's own child can make a parent anxious enough. Try looking after the welfare for upwards of 450 boys at one time, and it can be downright frightening. That was what faced the staff of the Alabama Boys' Industrial School, and if the gravity of that responsibility had not hit home immediately with Elizabeth Johnston and her sister board members, it soon would.

At the beginning, the boys' healthcare did not seem to be a major issue. A local physician, Dr. J. N. Killough, volunteered to attend to most of the school's medical needs at no charge. Any major illnesses or injuries were handled by taking the boys to one of the local hospitals. This tranquility did not last for long, as the third year brought a change of fortune. Mrs. Johnston wrote the governor:

> It has been a much more trying year than either of the preceding years. We have been called upon to chronicle our first death. Mason _____ was taken with fever; at first it seemed to be malarial, but developed into typhoid. After several weeks of sickness, during which he was carefully nursed, he died and was buried at Woodlawn.
>
> Quite a few of our boys were sick for a number of days, and two more occupied our sick room for four weeks. Three more were cared for at the hospital for two weeks. Dr. Killough, our faithful physician, came at our call night and day without any compensation other than a consciousness of doing good where his services were greatly needed."[1]

The physical condition of the students was good during Colonel Weakley's first year (1905). "The general health of the pupils has been excellent, and we are truly thankful the grim visitor of death has not, by his appearance added any gloom of sorrow to our home. There have been no contagious diseases of any kind; in fact, it has not been necessary to call in our physician but once during the entire year, then it was a case of biliousness." This term, popular in the eighteenth and nineteenth centuries, could best be described today as an upset stomach.

"We attribute this excellent record to Providence, the strict habits of the children, and the watchful care of their teachers and instructors," he continued. "There is much that can be done in a sanitary way to further insure the health and well being of the School in general which should be given more than passing attention. Lack of funds has prevented us from making these improvements."[2]

Those words proved prescient the very next year (1906) as typhoid fever struck the campus. Weakley told of their ordeal in his remarks to the board:

> During the latter part of July one of the boys was so unfortunate as to contract a case of typhoid fever, from which we soon experienced quite an epidemic, fifteen boys in all taking the fever, beside a number of others who were sick at the same time, swelling the number to about twenty-three. This sickness was a great surprise to the school officers and members of the Executive Board, for the hand of Providence had safely guided the whole school through a year and four months of splendid health, necessitating calling our physician only once during the entire time, and as a consequence, we were not prepared in any manner for the terrible siege we were destined to undergo. Then, too, the fact that we had no hospital facilities, no place to isolate the patients, and our plumbing and sewerage system in very bad shape, added horror and complexity to our position.[3]

In her comments to the governor, Mrs. Johnston also showed the anguish from the situation:

> From this wave of prosperity we were plunged almost without warning into an epidemic of typhoid fever. Four of our teachers left in one week; Mrs. Weakley and child were ill, and with only one man and two

lady teachers, Mr. Weakley was absolutely at the mercy of the boys, and I trembled for our work. But the foundation had been well laid, close and firm, and the boys rose to the occasion and asked to be placed in the positions made vacant by retiring officers; they carried on the work of the institution until we could reorganize and secure more aid. With fifteen cases of fever, the incomparable fact remains that we did not lose a boy, and stamped out the epidemic in about five weeks. Dr. Killough was most acceptable as a physician and states that his success was largely due to the fact that the sick boys were absolutely obedient to his orders."

One tragedy from the epidemic deeply touched the institution—and Mrs. Johnston. "Death, the relentless one, did not pass us by, but took the lamb of our flock, little Mary Fryer Weakley, the most beloved member of our household. She has gone to that School where Christ Himself doth rule and we know it is well with the child." The child was Colonel and Mrs. Weakley's three-year-old daughter.[4]

In Weakley's own remarks about the loss, his immense grief was apparent, but also his abiding faith:

> The Great God in his wisdom did not deem it best to take one of these boys, but an Angel of the Darker Hue visited our own family circle, and after six weeks of patient suffering our dear little girl, the light of our lives, was gathered to her Father in that Celestial Home not made with hands. And now while we mourn for her and her glad winsome smile; and shouts of merry laughter will never cheer us more, we would not have her return, for she has finished the journey and paid that debt all mortals must pay—death. And though our days here may be few or many, we know that just beyond the calm, enrapturing vista of eternity, small hands are beckoning us, and an invisible voice is entreating us to so live that after our eyes are closed in death, and we have laid our wearied selves down to take that last sleep, that we must not go in fear and trembling like a galley-slave, but to believe that as we journey from the finite to the infinite—from the measurable to the immeasurableness—that when the scintillating sheen that veils the Great Beyond is gently lifted by the hand

of Omnipotent, that there shall suddenly burst on our blinded visions the Great White Throne of God; and once again we shall be face to face with her we loved so well.[5]

The tenth year of the school was also beset with some medical issues, but none as catastrophic as before. "This has been the record year so far as acute sickness," Dr. Killough reported. "There have been light epidemics of measles and La Grippe (the flu), but no deaths resulting from either. One patient developed tuberculosis after a relapse of measles, but probably had incipient tuberculosis before taking the measles. We have had only one death, that from appendicitis. The above, with the exception of minor cases, covers all our sickness for the past year."

Dr. Killough also touched on preventive measures that should be employed. "I do not know of anything more conducive to good health and pleasure than the cold shower baths that are now given before retiring, and recommend a continuance of same. Special attention should be given to clean hands and face, and would insist that finger nails be kept cut short, for I am sure abcesses of neck and scalp have been to a great extent produced by scratching with infected nails." Dr. Killough also echoed a call first made by Colonel Weakley several years earlier to build a small hospital to serve the campus.[6]

That plea was answered when the second floor of the Johnston Building was converted into a hospital ward, with two private rooms and a small operating room. Over the years, a dental clinic was added, along with whatever medical equipment the school could afford.[7]

The hospital would be overwhelmed by the 1918 influenza epidemic that hit the nation, including Birmingham and the Alabama Boys' Industrial School. Approximately 100 cases were recorded at the school from students and employees. Unaffected students as well as community volunteers helped to care for the sick.

One of those community volunteers, Corinne Chisholm, was a writer for the *Birmingham News*. Her admiration for the boys was obvious in the article she wrote about her experiences:

It has been my privilege in the week just passed to become acquainted with many of the boys of the Alabama Industrial School at East Lake, and let me tell you, I have never in my life met a more mannerly or more appreciative bunch. I went out there to help in the hospital while so many were sick with influenza, so I know the sick boys as well as the well boys. It is hard to tell which are the finer. About twenty of the well boys are working in the hospital, keeping things clean and waiting on the patients and the nurses. They work twelve or fifteen hours a day without complaint and never have to be told anything twice. Almost overcome one night by my amazement at the thoughtfulness and efficient helpfulness of the boys, I exclaimed, 'Are there any bad boys out here?' At that, the youngsters burst into gales of laughter, and that was the only answer I got. The sick boys never complain and our chief concern is to find out what they want. There are many long rows of beds full of boys, none of whom, I'm happy

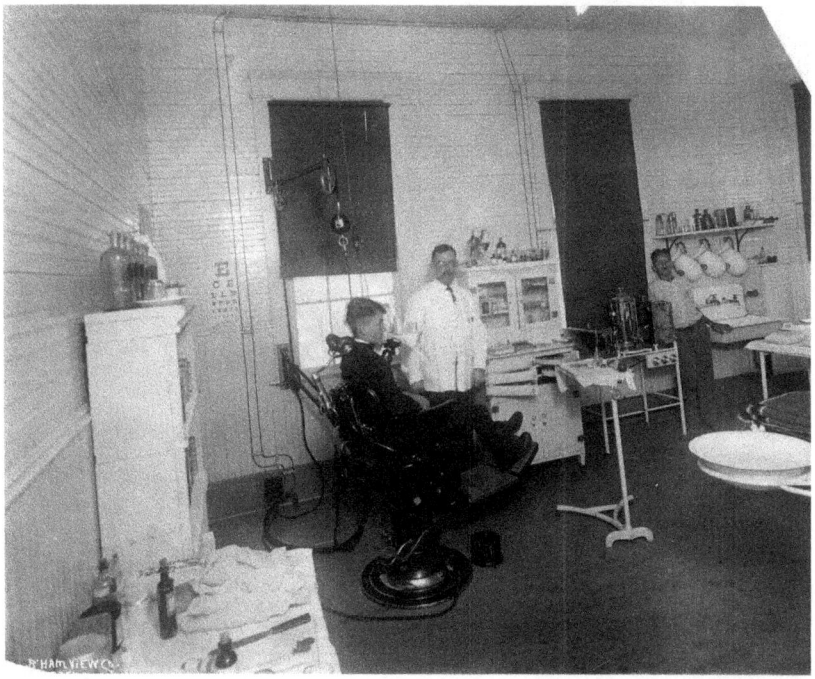

An ABIS student prepares for an examination while another waits his turn.

to say, is dangerously ill.⁸

Despite Chisholm's optimistic assessment, death did touch the student body again due to the epidemic, although incomplete records do not pinpoint the exact number of victims.

All was not life and death at the hospital. As one would expect with a school full of boys, there were the normal childhood illnesses and injuries. An exhaustive report from 1930–31 lists measles, mumps, chicken pox, hookworm, tonsillitis, hemorrhoids, constipation, trench mouth, burns, lacerations, and sprains. Also recorded was the removal of a needle from a boy's knee, with no explanation of how the needle got in the knee.⁹

These before and after photographs demonstrate the result of corrective surgery on a cross-eyed ABIS student.

The medical program at the school was not limited to responding to crises. Colonel Weakley and his staff prided themselves in being proactive, especially in regard to how physical conditions might impact behavior. In his papers, Weakley told of an operation performed on a young man with a double harelip, and how the success of that procedure dramatically changed the boy's personality and improved his school work. One boy had his crossed eyes properly aligned. Another student had several operations in the school's hospital to correct his clubfeet and enable him to walk normally. The youngster's delight with his new mobility led him to train in shoe repair at the school and open his own shoe shop in his hometown upon release.¹⁰

Such sophisticated operations were performed by some of the leading

Dr. J. N. Killough served ABIS for 25 years with little or no compensation. Numerous specialists in the Birmingham area also donated their services.

surgeons and specialists in Birmingham. Dr. Killough was so respected that he was able to enlist the best in the local medical community to donate their time and talent. Not the least among these benevolent physicians was Dr. Killough himself.

Weakley talked about the dedication of his friend and colleague at the time of the doctor's death:

> For over thirty years, Dr. Killough visited this school almost daily. In the early years when the school was struggling for existence, he gave his time, himself, and his energy without charge to relieve pain and suffering. Before the school was able to employ a trained nurse, Dr. Killough spent many nights in lonely vigils by the bed of some desperately sick boy. He was more than a doctor; he was a family physician; a healer of the body and soul.[11]

20

BOYS WILL BE BOYS

If someone had been at the helm of a home for mischievous boys for nearly half a century, it is a pretty safe bet he would have some stories to tell. Well, David Weakley certainly did, and he shared many of them in his personal papers. Some of the stories are humorous and provide a glimpse of the day-to-day life supervising hundreds of boys, while others are inspiring and give some idea of the simple rewards Weakley received from his lifelong undertaking.

Several of Weakley's favorite stories are linked by a practice that is still common even in today's correctional institutions. "Most boys at the school were usually given a nickname soon after arrival—sometimes in a matter of hours," he wrote. "It was usually based on appearance, stature, mannerism, or some unusual characteristic that was obvious."[1]

As an example, Weakley told of one boy from Mobile who entered the school one afternoon, and had earned his nickname before supper. It seems this new student considered himself somewhat of an authority on any subject, and did not mind sharing his knowledge whether it was requested or not. The boys soon dubbed him "Windy." The loquacious young man later became, quite fittingly, a radio announcer.[2]

Weakley described another youngster, whom his cohorts tagged as "Grasshopper," as being "jumpy, ever on the move—not mean—but a genuine nuisance." One day one of the feisty student's teachers came into Weakley's office to voice a little of her frustration with Grasshopper. As she plopped down in an inviting chair, she told her kindly boss of a recent revelation. "Mr. Weakley, I believe in the Bible more and more every day. You know I have Grasshopper in my class, and the Bible says, 'The Grasshopper shall become a burden,' and he is, and the prophecy has not failed."[3]

Another young man got his nickname out of his desperation. The boys, of course, were not allowed to have tobacco, yet a few of the fellows always seemed to have a little tucked away somewhere. A new resident at the school, a tall, lanky teenager from the country, had not yet learned how to acquire the precious commodity. One day he saw another student with a plug of tobacco and began begging for a share. After repeated rejections, he finally pleaded for his classmate to please give him just a "smidgen," and in so doing, earned a nickname that would last for years.[4]

The superintendent received a visitor on one occasion who was very interested in the nicknames the boys doled out to their mates. The lady was a professor of psychology at a noted university, and she was researching what she believed to be the negative, stigmatizing effects of nicknames within institutions. She believed that the use of such names was severely damaging to a youngster's self-esteem and should not be allowed in such a facility. Weakley admitted in his papers that he was somewhat skeptical of her theory, but tried to placate the professor by assuring her that the use of nicknames at his school was minimal and certainly not harmful. The guest seemed quite pleased and promised Weakley that she would mention his school and its enlightened leader in her upcoming book.

After some further discussion, Weakley's caller got up to leave. As Weakley escorted her to the door, a little boy entered the lobby. The professor greeted him warmly, patted him on the head and remarked, "Why young man, you must be the smallest boy in the school."

"Naw, ma'am," the boy replied politely, "ole Pole Cat is littler than me."

With some chagrin, Weakley confessed in his papers that the school was probably not mentioned prominently in her new book after all.[5]

Weakley recalled another visit from a college professor that had a much more positive ending. The woman was a faculty member at renowned Columbia University and she came to Birmingham specifically to meet the longtime superintendent and to see his school. One of her former students had been a resident at the school and had told her of an object lesson that Weakley had once used that had helped mold the young man into the disciplined learner he became.

The young man had always been bright and studious, but somewhat careless in his habits and badly in need of a little dose of responsibility. One

These two ABIS students, pictured near the spring that supplied the campus with water, were no doubt typical of the hundreds that passed through the school during Colonel Weakley's tenure. Their stories could range from the comical to the tragic.

A boy's day was filled with school, vocational training, work, military drill, and athletics. These boys also found a little time for relaxation.

afternoon he had been sent to the woods to cut some firewood and when he had finished his chore, he left behind the crosscut saw he had been using. Weakley sent him to retrieve it and ordered that he keep it in his possession until he told him otherwise—the saw was to accompany him to school, to the dining hall, to the playground, and even to bed at night. When the boy eventually left ABIS, he entered Columbia and had an outstanding record. The professor had complimented her student on how painstaking he was in his work, and he told her the story of the saw.

As Weakley talked with his protégé's professor, he sheepishly conceded that his methods might not meet with most educators' approval. She kindly told him, "I wish more of my boys had carried crosscut saws."[6]

Some of Weakley's stories carried no such moral but give a heartwarming picture of the innocence of the times. One boy sent to the school from a rural area could neither read nor write. One day he received a letter from his girlfriend back home, but he was at a quandary as to how he could get his true love's message given his inability to read. He finally arrived at a brilliant solution: "I'll give you a nickel to read the letter," he told one of his classmates, "but you will have to let me put my fingers in your ears so you can't hear what she says."[7]

A group of boys decided one day that they likewise would not let a minor problem deter them. Mr. and Mrs. Weakley had made a quick trip into the city, and the boys were left behind to cook some stew while the couple was away. A large caldron was simmering on the wood stove, when the flue came loose where it connected to the ceiling. One of the boys decided to put the paddle they were using to stir the stew across the top of the pot so he could stand on it to reach the flue. As he carried out this delicate procedure, his foot slipped on the greasy paddle and he fell into the boiling stew. Thankfully, his boots and military leggings prevented serious injury.

When the Weakleys returned, one of the tykes ran to meet them with the news of what had happened during their absence. After getting the other pertinent details and being assured that the young repairman was not injured, Weakley inquired about the stew, which, due to the fall, had now been seasoned with boot leather, mud, and other added ingredients. "Us et it," the informant replied without reservation.[8]

Food was at the heart of another story Weakley told about one of the boys on the kitchen staff. This youngster had a particular fondness for desserts, and had concocted a specialty he called "chocolate crony." The young cook was so proud of his sweet invention that it became an almost daily item on the school menu. When the boy left ABIS, he enlisted in the Army, and Weakley lost contact with him until the day the superintendent visited an Army installation on school business. The commanding officer invited Weakley to lunch at the base, and as they entered the mess hall, Weakley ran into his old kitchen boy. They had exchanged pleasantries and talked about old times for a few moments when Weakley jokingly asked if they were having chocolate crony. A somewhat awkward smile was the only response. Weakley bade him goodbye and took his seat alongside his host. Sure enough, as he opened the menu, his attention was drawn toward the day's special—"Chocolate Crony."[9]

Chefs were not the only professionals turned out by the school. There are accounts of ministers, teachers, attorneys, businessmen, musicians, and scores of craftsmen. Sometimes the process of assisting a student in reaching the pinnacle of his profession required quite a lot of understanding on the part of Weakley. He wrote of Jim, who was mechanically inclined and particularly liked tinkering with old cars. Jim persuaded Weakley to let him try to fix a problem the superintendent was having with his car, and he began the project late one afternoon. When Weakley checked on his progress the next morning, he found the young mechanic had worked all through the night removing the motor from the vehicle and had strewn it across the garage floor. Although somewhat perturbed, Weakley showed his usual patience and inquired about the diagnosis. Jim casually replied that the car "needed new rings and a valve job." In due time, he had all the parts back in their proper place and Weakley found "the old car ran perfectly."[10]

Another success story was a bit more serene. A boy was brought to the school by his uncle because he could not keep him at home. On most occasions, he was found at East Lake Park listening to the organ music of the merry-go-round. His interest in music flourished at ABIS, where he joined the band and became particularly adept at playing the cornet. After graduation, he studied music at a small college and later performed with professional orchestras around the country. One Christmas Eve years later, the Weakleys were in their living room listening to a national radio program when the host made the following announcement: "Next on the program will be a cornet solo, 'The Holy City,' by Mr. _____ dedicated to Mr. and Mrs. David Weakley, Birmingham, Alabama."[11]

Perhaps the most enduring legacy left by any of the Weakley-era students was that of the very first student, Jimmie _____. It has already been recounted how Jimmie's quick thinking allowed him the honor of being the first student admitted to the school. There's no doubt that Jimmie proved a little difficult for C. D. Griffin to manage in the early days of the school. What really needs to be told, however, is how Jimmie's story ended.

Jimmie "was among those we sent to Auburn in the fall of 1907," Weakley wrote. "He was handsome, intelligent and possessed a wonderful personality. He was an excellent student, and almost a genius in mathematics. He was an accomplished musician and an excellent printer.

"After completing his studies at college, he enlisted as a musician in the Marine Corps at the time we were building the Panama Canal. Due to his ability, he was soon promoted to director of a regimental Marine Band. He returned to the Alabama Boys' Industrial School later as instructor in printing and editor of the *Boys' Banner*. He resigned at the outbreak of World War I, and rejoined the Marine Corps. In due time, he was promoted to Captain and was killed in the Battle of Belleau Wood. The first boy to enter the Alabama Boys Industrial School was the first to give his life in the defense of his country."[12]

21

END OF AN ERA

On December 19, 1934, Elizabeth Johnston was resting at her campus cottage, Little Mount Vernon. She had only recently returned home from an operation intended to restore her failing eyesight. Even though she was not in good health, she was looking forward to Christmas and making plans for the various activities that would make the holidays more enjoyable for her boys.

After supper, Mrs. Johnston suffered some sharp pains, and her son Evans Johnston, who was staying with his mother while she convalesced, summoned a physician. By the time of his arrival, Mrs. Johnston was already feeling better, and he concluded that she was suffering from acute indigestion. She retired early, and when her son checked on her about midnight, he found her resting comfortably. During the night, however, death claimed the great lady. *The Boys' Banner*, in the eloquent prose of the day, described it like this:

> A messenger from the Grim Reaper called for Mrs. R. D. Johnston December 20, 1934 and carried her spirit to the mysterious realm where in dreamless slumbers she awaits the resurrection morn to greet those whom she loved.

Mrs. Johnston was eulogized at Birmingham's South Highland Presbyterian Church, which she and her husband had helped to organize. She was laid to rest with other members of her family in Charlotte, North Carolina.

Accolades poured in from all quarters. *The Banner* concluded its tribute by saying,

> Mrs. R. D. Johnston is gone but to those who knew her, the memory of

her life and her deeds will never fade, but will live on and grow clearer. To have known her is a pleasure, and to have been privileged to have a part in the work she started is a benediction.[1]

The *Birmingham Age-Herald* was effusive in its praise in a Christmas Eve editorial:

> Rarely does one have the satisfaction of rounding out a long and full life as did Mrs. R. D. Johnston, dying upon the campus of the institution which had its origin in her mind and will and its fulfillment in countless lives made straight and right by its ministrations. The Alabama Boys' Industrial School was her creation. It remains her monument, though her body rests in the state of her nativity.
>
> Mrs. Johnston's mortal remains are buried elsewhere. Her living memorial is here in the city and state of her adoption. Here her children arise and call her blessed, children of other mothers but of her shaping, children warped by circumstance and rescued by her handwork, children yet unborn, yet to stumble, and yet to be given a rebirth of hope and competence. Thus passeth an exalted woman and radiant prophetess of a better day for the buffeted children of men.[2]

David Weakley, the man by her side for twenty-nine years in their mutual labor of love, also expressed his appreciation:

> I think I know something of her matchless courage, her love for humanity, and the tact and wisdom which she so effectively used to overcome the many obstacles she so often encountered.
>
> It is given to few people to possess so many characteristics of greatness as did Mrs. Johnston, not the least of which were faith and humility. A faith that transcended things of this world and reached into eternity. A queenly humility that gave her the common touch that inspired confidence and enabled her to influence the lives of people.
>
> One of her greatest assets was the power of oratory. When she spoke people listened and were convinced, and her well modulated voice enabled

Mrs. Elizabeth Johnston during the latter years of her fruitful life.

her to play upon the emotions of her listeners like a master musician on a cathedral organ, but she never used this gift unless she felt it was for the glory of her God.[3]

As pleased as Mrs. Johnston would have been by such acknowledgment, it was faint praise compared to that found in a letter from one of her boys before her death. Frank wrote:

> You do not know how proud I am to be here. Just think, you are the mother of four hundred and fifty boys that we have here now. How wonderful it was of you to find such a beautiful place for a boy. Some of the boys would never had the opportunity on the outside that the boys here have. The boys here now and the ones in the past have classed you as their mother. Each and every one of us love you deep down in our hearts. When you talk to us on Sundays in Chapel, it makes me feel as though I owe something to you. Since you have been talking to us, I seem to be a changed boy. I certainly appreciate all that you have done for me and hope you will soon be back for we miss you.[4]

After Mrs. Johnston's death, Colonel and Mrs. Weakley continued their work at the school for another fourteen years, announcing their retirement in 1948 to coincide with the school's fiftieth anniversary. In his final report, the retiring superintendent was reflective:

> As I view the past from a distance of forty-three years and remember the trials and starving period we went through, I realize more than ever that it required a lot of patience and determination to overcome the almost insurmountable barriers that beset our way. As I contemplate and look over the beautiful campus and view the modern buildings, and especially as I call to mind the many thousands of boys who have left the school and who have developed into honest, worthwhile citizens, I feel that whatever the price, whatever the disappointments, that the time spent in building this school has been a worthwhile job.
>
> Mrs. Weakley and I are now retiring from the field of activity in which we have labored for half a century. We have made mistakes, and we realize that neither sorrow nor prayer can efface these mistakes, and that regrets will not atone for them, but whatever our shortcomings, we should like for those who remember us to forget what is best forgotten,

Elizabeth Johnston and David and Katherine Weakley stand outside Little Mount Vernon, Mrs. Johnston's retirement home on the ABIS campus.

and to remember what is best remembered, and that we may be judged not for what we were, but for what we should liked to have been.⁵

Weakley had no reason to worry about how they would be judged. The two local newspapers heaped praise upon the couple for their decades of service. *The Birmingham Post-Herald* offered this opinion:

> It is impossible to appraise accurately the contribution which Col. and Mrs. D. M. Weakley have made to their community and their country during the 43 years they have devoted to the ABIS. There is no yardstick by which one might measure the precious human values with which they have dealt. And yet we know, as do scores of friends who assembled at the school yesterday to pay tribute to these two fine people, that they have left their mark upon the lives of thousands of boys who have left the school to become responsible, upstanding citizens. We know that they have helped to build an institution which in years to come will continue to be an important influence in our state. They have been good and faithful servants, and to them all of us are deeply in debt.⁶

The Birmingham News added its own assessment:

> The scene was Roebuck; the time 43 years ago. To a log cabin school only seven years old came a young couple from Tennessee where they had been teaching together in an industrial school in Nashville. Now they were to take over management of this Alabama institution, organized in 1898 after a public spirited woman, the late Mrs. R. D. Johnston, had obtained a $3,000 donation from the legislature.
>
> The outlook must have been rather bleak, back in those early days with only the small log cabin, no trees or grass and just the barren land surrounding the school. But this did not daunt the young couple from Tennessee. They loved boys and knew how to get along with them, and must have been confident that they could make a success of their new work.
>
> Sunday at the ABIS the people of this state will pay fitting tribute to the long and excellent service of that teacher and his wife when they

Colonel David Weakley served forty-three years as ABIS superintendent.

honor Col. and Mrs. David M. Weakley in two special ceremonies at the school. As superintendent and matron, respectively, Col and Mrs. Weakley saw the humble cabin in which they started their work replaced by the present modern, efficient plant valued at $1,500,000.

They have seen the bare ground converted into smooth, tree-shaded lawns, the trees all planted by Mrs. Weakley, and they have seen their school develop into one of the foremost institutions of its kind in the South.

But the Weakleys have seen much more than these material things. They have watched, through the years, the progress of the boys who have come and gone, more than 7,000 of them, and have noted with pride the record many of them made in the outside world. The Weakleys don't think of these boys as delinquents, but as maladjusted. And it has been their job to help these boys find themselves and make of themselves good citizens.

How well Colonel and Mrs. Weakley have succeeded in their efforts along that line is attested by the record of their former pupils and the esteem in which this beloved couple is held today throughout Alabama. Now, after 43 years in a real labor of love, the Weakleys are retiring from the school. But they will not be idle. They plan to travel and visit former pupils and Col. Weakley will write of his experiences as a teacher. It should make interesting reading. The News is happy today in joining with the people of this state in offering its felicitations to this devoted couple."[7]

Regrettably, all of the plans the couple had for their retirement did not come to fruition. Mrs. Weakley died less than a year later.[8] Colonel Weakley began compiling his thoughts for a book, but never finished. Thankfully, those papers remain and were used as source material throughout this book. It is not the book he intended, but hopefully it can help to bring some long overdue recognition to this couple and the school they loved.

Colonel Weakley himself enjoyed a long retirement and did in fact keep his promise to visit the school regularly. He passed away in July 1971 at age ninety-three.[9]

22

Change

With David Weakley's retirement in 1948, there was a changing of the guard at the Alabama Boys' Industrial School. It had always been Weakley's hope that "one of his boys" would succeed him, and that dream was realized when former student J. B. Hill was named the school's superintendent.

Hill was indeed one of the most accomplished young men that the school ever produced. He was a graduate of Birmingham-Southern College with a degree in history and sociology and later received his master's degree in social work from Tulane University. Hill had also built an impressive resume in social work with the Methodist church, the juvenile court, and the American Red Cross.[1]

Life at the school during much of Hill's tenure was not remarkably different than that under his mentor. As late as 1964, the school still had its concert band, the *Banner*, a high school-level sports program, a farm, and an array of trades.[2] During Hill's twenty years at the helm, a gymnasium, three dormitories, and Hill Hall were added to the campus.[3]

John Carr was superintendent of the school during its most tumultuous period from 1967 until 1975.[4] The changes were not altogether by design, nor were they due to any neglect on the part of Carr. A tidal wave of change occurred in the state and nation during the 1970s that carried the school with it. Juvenile justice was receiving more attention than ever before, as indicated by Congress' creation of the Office of Juvenile Justice and Delinquency Prevention. This new federal agency enacted new policies, standards, and recommendations that drastically changed how states dealt with troubled youth. The Alabama Department of Youth Services was created during this period as a response to these federal mandates, and in 1975 the department assumed control of not only ABIS, but Chalkville and Mt. Meigs as well. No longer would each school have its own board of directors and manage its own affairs. ABIS's name was changed to Alabama Youth Services–Roebuck Campus.[5]

The nationwide civil rights movement also affected Alabama's juvenile institutions. ABIS had admitted its first black youth on March 26, 1970, in response to a court order requiring the school to racially integrate its student population. Another court order during this period established that the school's age range should be set at twelve to fourteen years of age, with older boys of both races being sent to Alabama Youth Services–Mt. Meigs, which had previously been exclusively for black boys.[6]

The reclassification of Alabama's juvenile institutions also led to programmatic changes. With the focus of the renamed Roebuck campus now being younger boys, the school's signature vocational program was largely dismantled, and its equipment was sent to Mt. Meigs. Hereafter, the school's only involvement in vocational education would be a class to "orient students to the world of work and help them make valid career choices."[7]

The emphasis of the school would now be on academics, with the ex-

McNeel School is one of the oldest buildings on campus, dating back to the Weakley era.

Graves Hall, originally the Mechanic Arts Building, now serves as an administration building.

Bush Chapel has been maintained, but the stately trees that surrounded it are a thing of the past.

pectation that on release most of the students would return to schools in their home communities.

Two other items relative to the recent history of the institution are worthy of note. In 1976, the Youth Services board voted to close the campus due to dwindling enrollment and other factors. Jefferson County, the City of Birmingham, and other local supporters filed suit to keep the campus open. Before the legal process reached a conclusion, the rising number of juvenile commitments to the Department of Youth Services led the board to reverse its decision, and within a year all three campuses were again operating at full capacity. In 1981, a joint resolution of the Alabama legislature renamed the institution as the Alabama Youth Services–Vacca Campus in recognition of Senator Pat Vacca, an advocate and ally of the school for more than thirty years. [8]

In the sixty-plus years after Colonel Weakley's retirement, there had been seven superintendents at the campus as of early 2014. The physical appearance of the campus has changed significantly since the Weakley days. From a high point of some thirty buildings, the campus now has only ten, with only three remaining from the Weakley era. Fencing and other security measures were added to the campus in 1991.[9]

The institution's population is much smaller today. In 1931, the average population was more than 450 boys, with approximately 650 total boys served during the year.[10] Today, the typical headcount is around 66 boys on a given day, with about 200 total youths housed during the entire year. The reduction is not because of any decline in juvenile delinquency, but rather due to an emphasis on probation and other local community programs instead of institutionalization.[11]

Today the school offers a sophisticated array of programs to deal with the problems of juvenile offenders. Short and long-term chemical addiction programs are provided, as well as classes in violence prevention and anger management. Athletic competition between the institution and other high schools has largely been replaced by intramural sports. Epiphany Ministries, a private ecumenical Christian ministry for young men and women housed in the juvenile justice system, is active on the campus.[12] The institution also has a chaplain who assists with the spiritual needs of the residents. Sadly, the beautiful Bush Chapel is no longer used to the fullest extent due to the security concerns presented by bringing large segments of the population together at one time.[13]

Much of the day-to-day activity on campus revolves around the academic program, housed in the Adele Goodwyn McNeel School. The academic program is a component of the Alabama Department of Youth Services school district, which functions under the same rules and regulations as any other public school system. The school day is divided into seven periods, with emphasis on the four core subjects of English, mathematics, social studies, and science. Because the boys are functioning at such varied levels, an individual educational service plan is developed for each student. The school is currently staffed with thirteen instructors, a principal, a counselor, a media specialist, and a psychometrist.[14]

Noticeably absent from the daily routine on campus is any semblance of the physical labor that Weakley felt was so crucial in turning boys into men. Working on the farm, assisting in the construction of buildings, and doing maintenance are a thing of the past. The culprit is a system burdened with endless regulations and frozen by the fear of litigation.

"The boys have not been allowed to work doing maintenance and the like for the last five to ten years, basically because of the regulations that are in place and liability issues," Superintendent James Thomas (2008–) explained. "The only way you can do it is if you have all the right safety requirements in place, and it just got to be a real hassle. It almost got to the point that we had to have one person supervising each boy, watching them to make sure they weren't doing anything dangerous."[15]

As dramatic as these changes have been, they are matched by the stark differences in the boys that are sent to the school and the problems that accompany them. The primary clientele today are young males between the ages of twelve and fifteen, although there are some exceptions. Today, more than 60 percent of the youths served by Vacca in a typical year are fourteen and fifteen years of age.[16] In 1910, nearly 60 percent were sixteen and seventeen years old.[17] Obviously, much of this difference comes from the institution's change in mission, but national trends also show that today's juvenile offenders are younger than ever before.[18]

The modern architecture of Smith Hall is energy efficient and more conducive to security.

The emphasis at DYS Vacca has shifted more toward security, as evidenced by Weakley-Underwood Hall.

The interior of Weakley-Underwood Hall is reflective of a medium security institution.

The podular design of Smith Hall allows for maximum surveillance of residents.

DYS Vacca Campus is almost completely devoid of trees due to the passage of time and the need for better security.

More remarkable than the age change has been the difference in the nature of the offenses committed by the boys sent to the institution. In 1910, the leading crimes were larceny, incorrigibility, gambling, disorderly conduct, and truancy.[19] One hundred years later, the most common offenses at the institution were robbery, burglary, larceny, assault, and drug crimes.[20] These statistics clearly show that yesterday's foolhardy, mischievous, adolescent behavior has escalated into serious, violent, criminal activity.

It is also worth noting that two-thirds of the current residents of this formerly all-white institution are now African American,[21] a percentage that closely approximates Alabama's adult prison population.[22]

Another difference in the two institutions is the length of time that boys stayed at the institution a century ago compared to today. A report from 1910 showed that most of the boys were ordered to stay at the school from their time of commitment until their eighteenth birthday, although parole was granted for exemplary behavior.[23] Certainly, most of the boys left the school before reaching adulthood, but it is obvious even from the anecdotal records left by Griffin and Weakley that many of the boys did stay for several years—ample time to get rid of some bad habits and replace them with some good ones. By contrast, the typical stay at Vacca today is four to six months.[24]

There have also been changes of a more subtle nature, such as the attitudes of the boys confined there. Carolyn Turner has been a counselor at the school since 1974, and she has seen significant attitudinal change even during her tenure. "In general, students now are harder to reach," she stated. "It's harder to get them to focus on change. They're more satisfied. They think it's okay that they're robbing and stealing. They have no remorse; they don't regret what they've done."[25]

Several factors have fueled this attitude, but one stands out above the rest. "Drugs have had the greatest impact," Turner concluded.[26] Superintendent Thomas bolstered her argument with his estimate that 80 percent of Vacca students have had some involvement with illegal drugs.[27]

The Johnston Administration Building on the DYS Vacca campus is a tribute to the school's founder.

Alabama Youth Services–Vacca Campus is very different from the school that was founded over 100 years earlier as the Alabama Boys' Industrial School. There are new programs, modern buildings, and highly educated professionals. The boys who come there have problems that would have confounded even the astute Colonel Weakley. What remains constant, however, is the school's steadfast devotion to helping troubled boys change.

Epilogue

Elizabeth Johnston and David Weakley were not the first to be concerned about the plight of wayward children. The care of what would today be called juvenile delinquents began in the earliest years of America's colonial period. In that day, even the criminal justice system for adults was sparse, with only a small collection of sheriffs, magistrates, and citizen watchmen to maintain order. Parents, therefore, were the first line for dealing with rebellious children. Youthful lawbreakers between the ages of seven and fourteen were normally sent home for their parents to administer a harsh whipping. Those who persisted in such behavior would be subject to the same corporal punishment given to an adult. Anyone fourteen and over was considered an adult and treated as such by the local authorities.[1]

When incarceration was introduced for adult criminals in Pennsylvania in 1790, it did not take long for a similar concept to appear for wayward youth. In 1825, a group of Quaker reformers opened the House of Refuge in New York City for six boys and three girls. The premise was that certain families were no longer able to provide the instruction and discipline that their children needed, and it was the state's responsibility to intercede. Harsh discipline, menial labor, and moral training became the order of the day. The movement grew in popularity throughout the first half of the nineteenth century, and similar facilities appeared in Philadelphia, Boston, and most major cities. New York State had twenty-seven such institutions by 1850.[2] The institutions not only grew in number, but in size. The original House of Refuge in New York grew from its original nine children to more than a thousand youths. One juvenile justice scholar called it "indistinguishable from an adult prison."[3]

A reform movement that began in the mid-nineteenth century had a profound influence on the care of youth. Comprised of middle-class women, clergy, academicians, and charity workers, the Child Savers were Progressive Era reformers who were concerned about the poverty, crime, and parental neglect to which children were being exposed in American cities. The Child Savers sought to intervene in the lives of these young people and restore them to a more wholesome environment. They advocated moving away from the large, prison-like institutions that characterized the houses of refuge toward cottages found in more rural environments, and they pushed for vocational training rather than menial labor. Their creations became known as reform schools or industrial schools.

Whether Elizabeth Johnston's motivations put her in the same company as the Child Savers is debatable. Some view the Child Savers as trying to recast poor little children into their own image to save American society as they knew it.[4] Johnston, on the other hand, seemed to be driven more by the specter of boys being forced to endure the harsh realities of adult prison. At any rate, her creation, the Alabama Boys' Industrial School, comes much closer to the reform school model than that of the house of refuge.

The idea of incarceration as a redress for criminal behavior in Alabama first surfaced in the 1830s, just a few years after Pennsylvania gave birth to the United States' first penitentiary. Following a few years of haggling in the state legislature, the Alabama State Penitentiary was opened in Wetumpka in 1842.[5] Since the first juvenile code would not be enacted in the state until 1907, boys were sentenced to the new prison right along with men if their crimes were sufficiently serious. One study found that before 1900 seven boys under the age of eighteen were executed in Alabama.[6]

The legislature's reasons for establishing its penitentiary were not much different than those of other states. Legislator Benjamin F. Porter, the "Father of the Alabama Penitentiary," touted its punitive value and capacity to keep dangerous criminals away from society.[7] Others praised its ability to reform criminals. Last, but not least, was the call for treating one's fellow human beings in a more humane manner than the severe whippings called for in the state's penal code. Such concern seems somewhat contradictory in light of the atrocity of slavery, but as Ward and Rogers put it, white Southerners seemed to have the ability to "compartmentalize their humanitarian concepts" when it came to that issue.[8]

Despite such promise, Alabama's new penitentiary was plagued by poor management from the beginning. After only five years of state administration, the 1846 legislature authorized the penitentiary's operation to be leased to the individual submitting the best bid.[9] Only a year later, the famous prison reformer Dorothea Dix of Massachusetts visited the institution and was not impressed. She found it to be "among the second class of Prisons in the South and West."[10] Although there were occasional signs of hope, no real changes occurred until after the Civil War.

After 1865, there was a distinct turning point, but for the worse. The legislature stipulated that leased inmates must do their work away from the institution, thus opening the door to the convict lease system. Convicts would be leased for their labor to railroad, timber, and mining companies, among others. Although inspectors were appointed to make sure the system ran smoothly, the convict lease system was fraught with problems ranging from cruelty to political corruption.[11] It was during the 1890s, in one of these mines filled with adult convicts, Elizabeth Johnston discovered the boy who would break her heart as she went to teach her prison Bible class.

Her discovery could not have come at a better time. The United States was just entering what would come to be known as the Progressive Era, a period of social activism and government reform. Even though Alabama's convict lease system would endure until the 1920s, it was already under intense scrutiny due to some of the inspectors' reports. Who knows with certainty what motivated the Alabama legislature to finally listen to Mrs. Johnston's pleas regarding the need for a boys' school, but the fact that they were already under increasing pressure concerning the state's penal system had to play to her advantage.

There may have been other factors at work as well. One writer has suggested that in some Southern states, what some would view as an act of benevolent social welfare really might have been a veiled attempt at social control. Perhaps the legislature was not as concerned with engaging in an act of kindness for these disadvantaged boys as it was in keeping them under a tight rein.[12] Nevertheless, it was an improvement over what the boys had been enduring.

Although some have found it surprising at this point in history that the

Alabama legislature was moved to action by a female, one writer thinks it makes perfect sense. A study of the Progressive Era in Georgia found that women were effective reformers in child welfare because their involvement seemed such a natural extension of their female role and did not come across as threatening to the male power structure. They were not stepping out of place; on the contrary, they were using their positions as wives and mothers to help enforce the social order.[13]

Even when the legislature created ABIS, they were not lavish with their expenditures. It was always a struggle for Mrs. Johnston and Colonel Weakley to get the state appropriations they needed. A 1918 report indicated that Alabama ranked fortieth out of the forty-three states reporting in terms of expenditures per boy at the new industrial school.[14] The situation is not much better today. A 2008 report on juvenile institutions found that Alabama was twenty-fourth out of the twenty-eight states reporting in regard to per student expenditures. Some citizens would applaud the state for its efficiency; others would say it shows a decided lack of interest when it comes to caring for the state's so-called "bad boys."[15]

Other issues come to light when considering the formation of the Alabama Boys' Industrial School. Was Mrs. Johnston unconcerned about black boys and intentionally omitted them from her new school? Once again, the answer is merely speculative, but several inferences can be drawn from what is known about the times. First of all, the Alabama penal system was largely white until after the Civil War, with the only exception being "free blacks." Although this changed during Reconstruction, it is doubtful that the percentage of black prisoners—adults or teens—had risen anywhere close to that of whites. For those black boys who were in the system, it would have been totally inappropriate for Mrs. Johnston to suggest in such a rigid, segregated society that they be placed in a school with white boys. Such an explanation does not make it right, but it was the way the South functioned at the time.

A 1910 report shows that Alabama was not much different than the rest of the nation—especially the South—on this subject. Of the approximate 25,000 offenders under age eighteen committed to the nation's juvenile institutions that year, only 10 percent were black. More than 70 percent of incarcerated black youths were still placed in jail or prison. Furthermore, Alabama was one of six Southern states that did not have a state-supported industrial school for delinquent youth of color at the time of the report, though that would soon change.[16] A separate institution for Alabama's black youths, initially called the Reformatory School, was started by the State Federation of Colored Women's Clubs in 1906 at Mt. Meigs. It started receiving state funding in the 1911–12 fiscal year. Like ABIS, that campus continues today as a fully integrated facility operated by the Department of Youth Services.[17]

The situation for females was and is somewhat different. Due to biological and sociological factors, males have always been more heavily involved in crime than females. Until recent years, most offenses committed by females in the United States were stereotypically based on gender. Even today, females account for only 14 percent of the juveniles in custody in the United States.[18] Nevertheless, even at the dawn of the twentieth century, Alabama had a need for residential care for young females. The Protestant Women of Birmingham opened a facility called the Rescue Home in 1909, which came under state control in 1911 and was renamed the State Training School for Girls. It moved to its present location in Chalkville in 1937.[19]

What made the Alabama Boys' Industrial School under Elizabeth Johnston and David Weakley so successful, and could such a program work in today's society? Adolescence is much more complicated today than a century ago. In 1900, some of the favorite toys for boys were wooden boats, tin cars, and train sets. Toy soldiers, marbles, and spinning tops also made the favorites' list. It is difficult to imagine any of those keeping today's adolescent boys occupied for very long. Radio did not become common until the 1920s, and television did not appear in most homes until the 1950s. The major sports of baseball, basketball, and football did not become widespread until the late 1800s. The life of a teenage boy was much different a century ago. Today's youth are more sophisticated and learn much faster; that can be a blessing and a curse.

After working in and teaching juvenile justice for over thirty-five years, this author sees two obstacles confronting today's youth that are much more daunting than those faced by boys in the early 1900s. The first is the change in the American family. An examination of the ABIS annual reports from 1925 and 1931 shows that more than 70 percent of the boys in residence had both natural parents at home. Today, fewer than 30 percent of delinquent youth live with two parents of any type, whether stepparents or natural parents.[20]

The second obstacle is the scourge of drugs among the nation's youth. *Banner* articles warned the boys about the dangers of tobacco. Tobacco is just the tip of the iceberg today. Numerous studies have shown that approximately 80 percent of juvenile offenders have had involvement with illicit drugs ranging from marijuana to cocaine to heroin.[21]

Given all of these factors, could a program like that at the early ABIS work with today's youth? For insight into this question, the author spoke with a longtime friend and colleague, Bobby Smith, who recently retired after forty years in childcare administration with the Alabama Sheriffs' Boys' Ranches and the Alabama Baptist Children's Homes. Particularly at the Boys' Ranch, Smith's approach was fairly reminiscent of the early days of ABIS, with an emphasis on discipline and vocational training.

At the ranch, the boys operated a working farm. Each boy attended school and spent time afterward attending to his daily chores. The boys lived in cottages with their "mom" and "pop" houseparents, just like a regular family. There were opportunities for play, and always time for worship. Smith is firm in his belief that such a program can work today, although he concedes there are some barriers, primarily the increasing number of government restrictions. Today, in his words, "the kids can't work, they can't go to church, they can't do anything." He also admits that such a program would not be effective for every youngster: "Some would accept it and others would not."

Still, Smith stands by the concept he used for so many years. "They learned how to make a living, they learned how to work, and they learned responsibility. It wasn't taught out of a book. They lived it. It wasn't easy, but it was good." The gentle giant—a former Mississippi State lineman—mentioned one final ingredient crucial for success: "We loved the kids, and they knew it."[22]

That seems to be the same prescription used by Mrs. Johnston and Colonel Weakley. They gave the boys the skills they needed to succeed in life, whether their interests were agriculture or auto mechanics. They provided the discipline the boys so desperately needed through strict rules, military drill, and even athletic competition. Finally, they wrapped it all in unconditional love. Without love, why else would a superintendent take an entire day to go fishing with a little boy who just had to get away or a board president give a child her husband's cherished Civil War medal? It was because they cared about the youngsters entrusted to them. Regardless of the program, plan, or strategy, it must be accompanied by love to be effective.

Juvenile justice is not easy today under the best of circumstances. A recent study found the recidivism rate for youth leaving an Alabama Department of Youth Services campus to be more than 70 percent[23]—just the opposite of what Weakley reported at the time of his retirement.[24] Given this discouraging report, it is not surprising that former Alabama Chief Justice Sue Bell Cobb demanded that "Our State's duty to our wayward children is when they come into care, they leave better off."[25]

To achieve that result, Alabama needs another generation of Elizabeth Johnstons and David Weakleys willing to devote their lives to Alabama's wayward boys and girls.

Notes

Chapter One
1. Mary Johnston Avery, *She Heard with Her Heart* (Birmingham: Birmingham Publishing Company, 1944), 2.
2. Ibid., 17.
3. Ibid., 7.
4. Ibid., 18.
5. Ibid., 17–18.
6. Ibid., 20-21.
7. Ibid., 30-31.
8. Ibid., 33-34.
9. Ibid., 35.
10. Ibid., 36.
11. Ibid., 72.
12. Ibid., 38-39.

Chapter Two
1. Avery, 41-42.
2. Ibid., 42.
3. Ibid., 43.
4. Ibid., 46-47.
5. Ibid., 54-55.
6. Ibid., 56.
7. Ibid., 59-61.
8. Ibid., 62.
9. Ibid., 62-63.
10. Ibid., 63.
11. Ibid., 64-65.

Chapter Three
1. Avery, 62.
2. ABIS reports, *Second Biennial Report* (Montgomery: State Printing Office for Alabama Industrial School for White Boys, 1903), 5-6.
3. ABIS reports, *Sixth Annual Report* (East Lake: Alabama Boys' Industrial School, 1905), 48-56.
4. Avery, 62.
5. *Sixth*, 48-49.
6. James Thomas, interview by author, Birmingham, June, 2010.
7. *Sixth*, 49.
8. *Acts of Alabama*, sec. 340 (1907).
9. *Sixth*, 49.
10. Ibid., 50.
11. Ibid., 51.
12. Ibid., 49.

Chapter Four
1. *Boys' Banner*, October 1948, "Forty-Third Anniversary of Dr. D. M. Weakley and Mrs. D. M. Weakley."
2. Avery, 69.
3. ABIS reports, *First Biennial Report* (Montgomery: State Printing Office for Alabama Industrial School for White Boys, 1900), 3-4.
4. Ibid., 3.
5. Avery, 74.
6. Ibid., 75.
7. Ibid., 75-76.
8. David Weakley Papers, 1961, Archives,

Birmingham Public Library, Birmingham, Alabama, 131.
9. Avery, 70.
10. Weakley, 132-133.
11. Avery, 71.

Chapter Five
1. Weakley, 130.
2. *First*, 4.
3. C. D. Griffin Diary, 1900-1901, Alabama Department of Archives and History, Montgomery, Alabama.

Chapter Six
1. Griffin.
2. ABIS reports, *Fifth Annual Report*, (East Lake: Alabama Boys' Industrial School, 1905), 6.
3. *Sixth*, 7.
4. Weakley, 2.
5. Ibid., 5.

Chapter Seven
1. Weakley, 252-253.
2. Ibid., 5-6.
3. Ibid., 253.
4. Ibid., 3.
5. Ibid., 4.
6. Ibid., 7.
7. Ibid., 8.
8. Ibid., 9.
9. Ibid., 9-10.

Chapter Eight
1. Weakley, 33.
2. *Second*, 11.
3. *Birmingham News*, Hugh M. Sparrow, "Boys' Industrial School Is Guide to Misguided," January 4, 1945.
4. Weakley, 130-131.
5. Ibid., 132.
6. Ibid., 14-16.

7. Ibid., 135-137.
8. Ibid., 138-139.
9. Ibid., 143.
10. Ibid., 148.
11. Ibid., 150.
12. Ibid., 154.
13. Ibid., 157.
14. Ibid., 152.
15. Ibid., 160-162.
16. Ibid., 162-163.
17. Ibid., 164-165.

Chapter Nine
1. *Birmingham Post-Herald*, Jane Aldridge, "His System May Be Wrong, but Colonel Gets Results," June 10, 1948.
2. *Fifth*, 1-2.
3. *Sixth*, 18.
4. ABIS reports, *Seventh Annual Report* (East Lake: Alabama Boys' Industrial School, 1907), 8.
5. *Birmingham News*, Allen Rankin, "He's Saved many from Jail, They've Paid Him in Gratitude," August 19, 1947.
6. Aldridge.
7. Rankin.
8. ABIS reports, *Thirty-First Annual Report*, (Birmingham: Alabama Boys' Industrial School, 1931), 14.
9. Sparrow.
10. Tom Foster, interview by author, Birmingham, Alabama, January 2011.

Chapter Ten
1. *Thirty-First*, 64.
2. *First*, 6.
3. Ibid.
4. *Second*, 19.
5. Ibid., 14.
6. ABIS reports, *Third Annual Report*, (East Lake: Alabama Boys' Industrial School, 1903), 4.

7. *Sixth*, 29.
8. Weakley, 25.
9. ABIS reports, *Twenty-Fifth Annual Report*, (East Lake: Alabama Boys' Industrial School, 1925), 15.
10. *Second*, 14.
11. *Sixth*, 30-31.
12. Weakley, 19-23.
13. Scott Dawsey, interview by author, Tuscumbia, Alabama, December, 2009.
14. Weakley, 19-21.
15. *Sixth*, 30.
16. Weakley, 18.
17. Ibid.
18. *Second*, 17.
19. *Third*, 4.
20. Weakley, 27.
21. ABIS reports, *Fifteenth Annual Report*, (East Lake: Alabama Boys' Industrial School, 1915), 13.
22. *Thirty-First*, 62.

Chapter Eleven
1. Sparrow.
2. Weakley, 40.
3. *Sixth*, 27.
4. *Fifteenth*, 13.
5. Weakley, 28.
6. Ibid., 24.
7. *Thirty-First*, 58.
8. Weakley, 24.
9. *Thirty-First*, 26.
10. *Twenty-Fifth*, 16.
11. *Thirty-First*, 32.
12. Weakley, 37.
13. Weakley, 38.
14. *Thirty-First*, 50.
15. Weakley, 29.

Chapter Twelve
1. Hastings Hornell Hart, *Preventive Treatment of Neglected Children* (New York: Russell Sage Foundation, 1910), 18.
2. *First*, 7-8.
3. *Second*, 12-13.
4. *Sixth*, 46-47.
5. Ibid., 34-35.
6. Ibid., 35.
7. Ibid., 46-47.
8. Ibid., 47.
9. Ibid., 35.
10. Ibid.
11. ABIS reports, *Twenty-Second Annual Report* (East Lake: Alabama Boys' Industrial School, 1922), 10.
12. Weakley, 35.
13. *Twenty-Fifth*, 14
14. Ibid.
15. *Thirty-First*, 34-35.
16. Sparrow.
17. *Thirty-First*, 39.

Chapter Thirteen
1. *Second*, 13.
2. Weakley, 8.
3. *Seventh*, 27-28.
4. Weakley, 10.
5. *Sixth*, 33.
6. Weakley, 39-40.
7. *Thirty-First*, 45.
8. *Sixth*, 41.
9. *Seventh*, 12.
10. Ibid.
11. *Sixth*, 40-41.
12. ABIS reports, *Ninth Annual Report* (East Lake: Alabama Boys' Industrial School, 1908), 24.
13. Weakley, 202.
14. Ibid., 20.
15. Rankin.

Chapter Fourteen
1. *Second*, 17.
2. *Sixth*, 6-7.
3. Ibid., 26.
4. Weakley, 61.
5. Ibid., 55-56.
6. ABIS reports, *Twenty-Seventh Annual Report* (Birmingham: Alabama Boys' Industrial School, 1927), 47.
7. *Thirty-First*, 53.
8. Weakley, 56-59.
9. Ibid., 61-62.
10. Ibid., 55-56.

Chapter Fifteen
1. Weakley, 65
2. Harry E. Allen, Edward J. Latessa, and Bruce S. Ponder, *Corrections in America*, 12th ed. (Upper Saddle River, New Jersey: Pearson Prentice Hall, 2009), 31.
3. ABIS reports, *Fourth Annual Report* (East Lake: Alabama Boys' Industrial School, 1904), 8-9.
4. Weakley, 64.
5. Ibid., 64-65.
6. *Woodlawn-East Lake News*, "Boys' Industrial School Great Asset in Training State's Misguided Youth," February 8, 1946.
7. Weakley, 64.
8. *Sixth*, 44.
9. Ibid., 5.
10. Ibid., 43-44.
11. Avery, 73.
12. Weakley, 69-70.
13. Ibid., 68.
14. Ibid., 72.
15. *Thirty-First*, 27-31.
16. Weakley, 72-73.
17. Rankin.
18. Weakley, 203-204.
19. Ibid., 75.
20. *Thirty-First*, 30.
21. Weakley, 74.
22. Avery, 73.

Chapter Sixteen
1. Griffin.
2. *Boys' Banner*, "Boys Enjoy Vitagraph Feature," March, 1924.
3. *Boys' Banner*, "Bible Class," October, 1924.
4. *Boys' Banner*, "Frazier, Lyons Wedding Event of August," September, 1936.
5. *Boys' Banner*, "Amateurs Begin Practice on the Grid," September, 1936.
6. *Boys' Banner*, "Football Team Sees Important Game at Legion Field," December, 1932.
7. *Boys' Banner*, "Harry Gilmer and Virgil Trucks Attend Big Football Banquet," December 14, 1945.
8. *Boys' Banner*, "Farm Report," October, 1924.
9. *Boys' Banner*, "Microscope Study Now Used in Classes," September 28, 1945.
10. *Boys' Banner*, "Laundry," March, 1924.
11. *Boys' Banner*, "Boys in Barber Shop Have No Time to Loaf," June, 1934.
12. *Boys' Banner*, "Billie," February, 1939.
13. *Boys' Banner*, "Campus Chatter," February, 1936.
14. *Boys' Banner*, "Comings, Goings, and Doings," November 27, 1945.
15. *Boys' Banner*, "Rakings," August, 1907.
16. *Boys' Banner*, "Sports," June, 1936.
17. *Boys' Banner*, "It's the Man Who Does Things," February, 1936.
18. *Boys' Banner*, "Don't Smoke, Boys," October, 1907.
19. *Boys' Banner*, "A Mistake Often Made," January, 1936.
20. *Boys' Banner*, "For What We Get We

Have to Pay," June, 1936.
21. *Boys' Banner*, "It Must Be Great," May, 1934.
22. *Boys' Banner*, "Just Around the Corner," April, 1934.
23. *Boys' Banner*, "Crazy Cracks," May, 1934.
24. *Boys' Banner*, "Spare Moments with the Jokemaker," October, 1932.

CHAPTER SEVENTEEN
1. *Birmingham News*, "City's Salesmen's Club to Conduct Campaign for ABIS School," September 15, 1940.
2. *Boys' Banner*, "Base Ball," September, 1907.
3. "Rakings."
4. "Base Ball."
5. *Boys' Banner*, "Basketball Season to Start," December, 1932.
6. *Boys' Banner*, "Golden Tornadoes Train," January, 1938.
7. *Boys' Banner*, "Sports Shots," December 14, 1945.
8. *Boys' Banner*, "Sports," November 27, 1945.
9. *Boys' Banner*, "Sports," January, 1939.
10. *Boys' Banner*, "Punt Formation," January, 1938.
11. *Boys' Banner*, "Jinx on Football," October, 1939.
12. "Salesmen's Club."
13. *Birmingham Post-Herald*, "Karnegay Wins Steak Dinner for Touchdown," November 6, 1945.
14. *Boys' Banner*, "Sports Shorts," November 27, 1945.

CHAPTER EIGHTEEN
1. Avery, 70-71.
2. *Second*, 17.
3. Griffin.
4. ABIS reports, *Twenty-Third Annual Report* (East Lake: Alabama Boys' Industrial School, 1923), 10.
5. Weakley, 107.
6. *Fifteenth*, 27.
7. Avery, 82.
8. Ibid., 79.
9. Weakley, 107-108.

CHAPTER NINETEEN
1. *Third*, 2-3.
2. *Sixth*, 27.
3. *Seventh*, 8-9.
4. Ibid., 2-3.
5. Ibid., 9-10.
6. ABIS reports, *Tenth Annual Report* (East Lake: Alabama Boys' Industrial School, 1909), 30-31.
7. Weakley, 135.
8. Ibid., 43-45.
9. *Thirty-First*, 40-44.
10. Weakley, 47.
11. ABIS reports, *Thirty-Second Annual Report* (Birmingham: Alabama Boys' Industrial School, 1932), 9-10.

CHAPTER TWENTY
1. Weakley, 195
2. Ibid., 196.
3. Ibid.
4. Ibid., 194.
5. Ibid., 192.
6. Ibid., 204-205.
7. Ibid., 208.
8. Ibid., 209.
9. Ibid., 210.
10. Ibid., 200-201.
11. Ibid., 212.
12. Ibid., 14.

Chapter Twenty-One
1. *Boys' Banner*, "Mrs. R.D. Johnston, Lover of Humanity," June, 1937.
2. ABIS reports, *Thirty-Fifth Annual Report* (Birmingham: Alabama Boys' Industrial School, 1935), 13-14.
3. Avery, 111-112.
4. Weakley, 276.
5. ABIS reports, *Forty-Eighth Annual Report*, (Birmingham: Alabama Boys' Industrial School, 1948), 22-23.
6. *Birmingham Post-Herald*, "Well Done," October 11, 1948.
7. *Birmingham News*, "The Way of the Weakleys," October 9, 1948.
8. Weakley, 268.
9. *Boys' Banner*, "Col. Weakley, Supt. Emeritus, Passes," August, 1971.

Chapter Twenty-Two
1. *Birmingham Post-Herald*, "One of the Boys Back to Head ABI School," April 15, 1948.
2. ABIS reports, *Annual Report 1963-64* (East Lake: Alabama Boys' Industrial School, 1964), 9-12.
3. Thomas.
4. Ibid.
5. Ibid..
6. ABIS reports, *Annual Report 1969-70* (East Lake: Alabama Boys' Industrial School, 1970), 3-4.
7. ABIS reports, *Annual Report 1973-74* (East Lake: Alabama Boys' Industrial School, 1974), 7.
8. Thomas.
9. Ibid.
10. *Thirty-First*, 14.
11. Thomas.
12. Department of Youth Services, "Vacca Campus," http://dys.alabama.gov/Vacca.html (accessed September, 2011).
13. Thomas.
14. Alabama Department of Youth Services, "McNeel School," http://dys.alabama.gov/mcneelschool.html (accessed September, 2011).
15. Thomas.
16. Allen Peaton, interview by author, Montgomery, Alabama, September, 2011.
17. U.S. Department of Commerce, Bureau of the Census, *Prisoners and Juvenile Delinquents in the United States 1910* (Washington, D.C.: Government Printing Office, 1918), 524.
18. Office of Juvenile Justice and Delinquency Prevention, "Easy Access to Juvenile Court Statistics: 1985-2011," http://www.ojjdp.gov/ojstatbb/ezajcs/ (accessed October, 2011).
19. *Prisoners and Juvenile Delinquents*, 506-508.
20. Peaton.
21. Ibid.
22. Alabama Department of Corrections, "Statistical Reports," http://www.doc.state.al.us/StatReports.aspx, (accessed October, 2011).
23. *Prisoners and Juvenile Delinquents*, 523.
24. Thomas.
25. Carolyn Turner, interview by author, Birmingham, Alabama, August, 2011.
26. Ibid.
27. Thomas.

Epilogue
1. Clemens Bartollas, *Juvenile Delinquency*, 12th ed. (Boston: Pearson Eduication, Inc., 2006), 17.
2. Peter C. Kratcoski and Lucille Dunn Kratcoski, *Juvenile Delinquency*, 5th ed. (Upper Saddle River, New Jersey: Pearson Prentice Hall, 2004), 80.
3. Larry Siegel and Brandon Welsh, *Juve-*

nile Delinquency: Theory, Practice, and Law, 11th ed. (Belmont, California: Wadsworth Cengage Learning, 2012), 476-477.
4. Ibid., 475-477.
5. Robert David Ward and William Warren Rogers, *Alabama's Response to the Penitentiary Movement, 1829-1865.* (Gainesville, Florida: University of Florida Press, 2004), 62.
6. M. Watt Espy and John Ortiz Smykla, *Executions In the United States 1608-2002, The Espy File*, http://www.deathpenaltyinfo.org/documents/ESPYstate.pdf (accessed July, 2011).
7. *Alabama's Response*, 5-6.
8. Ibid., 19-20.
9. Robert David Ward and William Warren Rogers, *Convicts, Coal, and the Banner Mine Tragedy.* (Tuscaloosa, Alabama: The University of Alabama Press, 1987), 28.
10. *Alabama's Response*, 98.
11. *Convicts*, 30-44.
12. John Wallenstein, "Laissez Faire and the Lunatic Asylum," in *Before the New Deal: Social Welfare in the South, 1830-1930*, ed. Elna C. Green (Athens, Georgia: The University of Georgia Press, 1999), 5.
13. Lee S. Polansky, "I Certainly Hope that You Will Be Able to Train Her: Reformers and the Georgia Training School for Girls," in *Before the New Deal: Social Welfare in the South, 1830-1930*, ed. Elna C. Green (Athens, Georgia: The University of Georgia Press, 1999), 140.
14. Department of the Interior, Bureau of Education, *Industrial Schools for Delinquents 1917-1918* (Washington D.C.: Government Printing Office, 1920), 31.
15. The Justice Policy Institute, "The Costs of Confinement: Why Good Juvenile Justice Policies Make Good Fiscal Sense," http://www.justicepolicy.org/Images/upload/09_05_REP-CostsOf-Confinement_JJ_PS.pdf (accessed July, 2011).
16. *Prisoners and Juvenile Delinquents*, 192.
17. Alabama Department of Youth Services, "Mt. Meigs Campus," http://dys.alabama.gov/Facilities/MtMeigsCampus.htm (accessed July, 2011).
18. Office of Juvenile Justice and Delinquency Prevention, "Female proportion of juveniles in residential placement, 2007," U.S. Department of Justice, http://www.ojjdp.gov/ojstatbb/corrections/qa08202.asp?qaDate=2007 (accessed July, 2011).
19. Alabama Department of Youth Services, "Chalkville Campus," http://dys.alabama.gov/Facilities/ChalkvilleCampus.htm (accessed July, 2011).
20. Curt Alfrey, "Juvenile Delinquency and Family Structure: Implications for Marriage and Relationship Education," National Healthy Marriage Resource Center, http://helathymarriageinfo.org/resource-detail/index.aspx?rid=3370 (accessed July, 2011).
21. Howard N. Snyder and Melissa Sickmund, *Juvenile Offenders and Victims: A National Report.* U.S. Department of Justice, Office of Juvenile Justice and Delinquency Prevention, (Washington D.C.: Government Printing Office, 1995), 64.
22. Bobby Smith, interview by author, Decatur, Alabama, June, 2011.
23. *Birmingham News*, Carla Crowder, "Study Finds 70% of Kids Sent to DYS Return to Trouble," August 5, 2005.
24. *Birmingham News*, John Atkins, "A Chapter in Reclaiming Alabama Youth Ends as the Weakleys Retire," October 8, 1948.
25. Crowder.

Bibliography

Acts of Alabama. Act 340, 1907.

Alabama Boys' Industrial School *Annual Reports: Third,* 1903; *Fourth,* 1904; *Fifth,* 1905; *Sixth,* 1905; *Seventh,* 1906; *Ninth,* 1908; *Tenth,* 1909; *Fifteenth Annual Report,* 1915; *Twenty-Second,* 1922; *Twenty-Third,*1923; *Twenty-Fifth,* 1925; *Twenty-Seventh,* 1927; *Thirty-First,* 1931; *Thirty-Second,* 1932; *Thirty-Fifth,*1935; *Forty-Eighth,* 1948; *1963-64,* 1964; *1969-70,* 1970; *1973-74,* 1974.

Alabama Department of Corrections, http://www.doc.state.al.us/reports.asp, (accessed October, 2011).

Alabama Department of Youth Services, Chalkville Campus. http://dys.alabama.gov/Facilities/ChalkvilleCampus.htm (accessed July, 2011).

Alabama Department of Youth Services, McNeel School, http://dys.alabama.gov/mcneelschool.html (accessed September, 2011).

Alabama Department of Youth Services, Mt. Meigs Campus. http://dys.alabama.gov/Facilities/MTMeigsCampus.htm (accessed July, 2011).

Alabama Department of Youth Services, Vacca Campus, http://dys.alabama.gov/Vacca.html (accessed September, 2011).

Alabama Industrial School for White Boys. *First Biennial Report,* 1900; *Second Biennial Report,* 1903.

Aldridge, Jane. "His System May Be Wrong, but Colonel Gets Results." *Birmingham Post-Herald,* June 10, 1948.

Alfrey, Curt. "Juvenile Delinquency and Family Structure: Implications for Marriage and Relationship Education." National Healthy Marriage Resource Center, http://healthymarriageinfo.org/resource-detail/index.aspx?rid=3370 (accessed July, 2011).

Allen, Harry E., Edward J. Latessa, and Bruce S. Ponder. *Corrections in America.* 12th ed. Upper Saddle River, New Jersey: Prentice Hall, 2009.

Atkins, John. "A Chapter in Reclaiming Alabama Youth Ends as the Weakleys Retire," *Birmingham News,* October 8, 1948

Avery, Mary Johnston. *She Heard with Her Heart.* Birmingham, Alabama: Birmingham Publishing Company, 1944.

Bartollas, Clemens. *Juvenile Delinquency,* 12th ed. Boston: Pearson Education, 2006.

Crowder, Carla. "Study Finds 70% of Kids Sent to DYS Return to Trouble," *The Birmingham,* August 5, 2005.

Dawsey, Scott. Interview by author, Tuscumbia, Alabama, December, 2009.

Espy, M. Watt and John Ortiz Smykla. "Executions in the United States, 1608-2002." The Espy File, http://www.deathpenaltyinfo.org/documents/ESPYstate.pdf (accessed July, 2011).
Foster, Tom. Interview by author, Birmingham, Alabama, January, 2011.
Griffin, C.D., Diary. Alabama Department of Archives and History, Montgomery, Alabama, 1900-1901.
Hart, Hastings Hornell. *Preventive Treatment of Neglected Children*. New York: The Russell Sage Foundation, 1910.
Kratcoski, Peter C. and Lucille Dunn Kratcoski. *Juvenile Delinquency*, 5th ed. Upper Saddle River, New Jersey: Pearson Prentice Hall, 2004.
Office of Juvenile Justice and Delinquency Prevention, http://www.ojjdp.gov/ojstatbb/ezajcs/, (accessed October, 2011).
Polansky, Lee S. "I Certainly Hope that You Will Be Able to Train Her: Reformers and the Georgia Training School for Girls." In *Before the New Deal: Social Welfare in the South, 1830-1930*. Edited by Elna C. Green, 138-159. Athens, Georgia: University of Georgia Press, 1999.
Peaton, Allen. Interview by author, Montgomery, Alabama, September, 2011.
Rankin, Allen. "He's Saved Many from Jail, They've Paid Him in Gratitude." *Birmingham News*, August 19, 1947.
Siegel, Larry and Brandon Welsh. *Juvenile Delinquency: Theory, Practice and Law*, 11th ed. Belmont, California: Wadsworth Cengage Learning, 2012.
Smith, Bobby. Interview by author, Decatur, Alabama, June, 2011.
Sparrow, Hugh M. "Boys' Industrial School Is Guide to Misguided." *Birmingham News*, January 4, 1945.
Birmingham News. "City Salesmen's Club to Conduct Campaign for ABIS School." September 15, 1940.
Birmingham News. "The Way of the Weakleys." October 9, 1948.
Birmingham Post-Herald. "Karnegay Wins Steak Dinner for Touchdown." November 6, 1945.
Birmingham Post-Herald. "One of the Boys Back to Head ABI School," April 15, 1948.
Birmingham Post-Herald. "Well Done." October 11, 1948.
The Boys' Banner. "Amateurs Begin Practice on the Gird." September, 1936.
The Boys' Banner. "A Mistake Often Made." January, 1936.
The Boys' Banner. "Base Ball." August, 1907.
The Boys' Banner. "Base Ball." September, 1907.
The Boys' Banner. "Baskeball Season to Start." December, 1932.
The Boys' Banner. "Bible Class." October, 1924.
The Boys' Banner. "Billie." February, 1939.
The Boys' Banner. "Boys Enjoy Vitagraph Feature." March, 1924.
The Boys' Banner. "Boys in Barber Shop Have No Time to Loaf." June, 1934.
The Boys' Banner. "Campus Chatter." February, 1936.

The Boys' Banner. "Col. Weakley, Supt. Emeritus, Passes." August, 1971.
The Boys' Banner. "Coming, Goings and Doings." November, 1945.
The Boys' Banner. "Crazy Cracks." May 1934.
The Boys' Banner. "Don't Smoke, Boys." October, 1907.
The Boys' Banner. "Farm Report." October, 1924.
The Boys' Banner. "Football Team Sees Important Game at Legion Field." December, 1932.
The Boys' Banner. 'Forty-Third Anniversary of Dr. D.M. Weakley and Mrs. D.M. Weakley." October, 1948.
The Boys' Banner. "For What We Get We Have to Pay." June, 1936.
The Boys' Banner. "Frazier, Lyons Wedding Event of August." September, 1936.
The Boys' Banner. "Golden Tornadoes Train." January, 1938.
The Boys' Banner. "Harry Gilmer and Virgil Trucks Attend Big Football Banquet." December 14, 1945.
The Boys' Banner. "It Must Be Great." May, 1934.
The Boys' Banner. "It's the Man Who Does Things." February, 1936.
The Boys' Banner. "Mrs. R.D. Johnston, Lover of Humanity." June, 1937.
The Boys' Banner. "Jinx on Football." October, 1939.
The Boys' Banner. Just Around the Corner." April, 1934.
The Boys' Banner. "Laundry." March, 1924.
The Boys' Banner. "Microscope Study Now Used in Classes." September 28, 1945.
The Boys' Banner. "Punt Formation." January, 1938.
The Boys' Banner. "Rakings." August, 1907.
The Boys' Banner. "Spare Moments with the Jokemaker." October, 1932.
The Boys' Banner. "Sports." June, 1936.
The Boys' Banner. "Sports." January, 1939.
The Boys' Banner. "Sports Shots." November 27, 1945.
The Boys' Banner. "Sports Shots." December 14, 1945.
The Espy File. http://www.deathpenaltyinfo.org/documents/ESPYstate.pdf
The Justice Policy Institute. "The Costs of Confinement: Why Good Juvenile Justice Policies Make Good Fiscal Sense." http://www.justicepolicy.org/images/upload/09_05_REP_CostsofConfinement_JJ_PS.pdf (accessed July, 2011).
Thomas, James. Interview by author, Birmingham, Alabama, June, 2011 and August, 2011.
Turner, Carolyn. Interview by author, Birmingham, Alabama, August, 2011.
U.S. Department of Commerce. Bureau of the Census. *Prisoners and Juvenile Delinquents in the United States 1910*. Washington D.C.: Government Printing Office, 1918.
U.S. Department of the Interior. Bureau of Education. *Industrial Schools for Delinquents 1917-18*. Washington D.C.: 1920.
U.S. Department of Justice. Office of Juvenile Justice and Delinquency Prevention. *Juvenile Offenders and Victims: A National Report* by Howard N. Snyder

and Melissa Sickmund. Washington D.C.: Government Printing Office, 1995.

Wallenstein, John. "Laissez Faire and the Lunatic Asylum." In *Before the New Deal: Social Welfare in the South, 1830-1930*, edited by Elna C. Green, 3-23. Athens, Georgia: University of Georgia Press, 1999.

Ward, Robert David and William Warren Rogers. *Alabama's Response to the Penitentiary Movement, 1829-1865*. Gainesville, Florida: University of Florida Press, 2004.

Ward, Robert David and William Warren Rogers. *Convicts, Coal, and the Banner Mine Tragedy.* Tuscaloosa, Alabama: University of Alabama Press, 1987.

Weakley, David, Papers. Archives, Birmingham Public Library, Birmingham, Alabama, 1961.

Woodlawn-East Lake News. "Boys' Industrial School Great Asset in Training State's Misguided Youth." February 8, 1946.

INDEX

A

Adele Goodwyn McNeel School 155, 158
African Americans xiii, 5, 9, 19, 31, 155, 161, 167
Alabama
 and black juveniles xiii
 Archives and History Department xii, xiii, 179
 juvenile court system of xi, 20
 legislature of 13–15, 18, 43, 48, 70, 151, 157, 165–167
 Pensions and Security Department xi
 prison system of xiii, 11, 12, 14, 20, 25, 58, 161, 165–168
 Youth Services Department. See Alabama Department of Youth Services
Alabama Baptist Children's Homes 169
Alabama Boys' Industrial School xi–xiii
 and academics 86–90
 and all-female board 13, 17
 and athletics 117–123
 and baking 77
 and band 98–105
 and barbering 77–78
 and blacksmithing 71–72
 and carpentry 66–71
 and farming 80–85
 and health 131–138, 157
 and military training 91–97
 and "motherly" influences 13, 16–20
 and painting 76–77
 and recreation 31, 33, 54, 55, 96, 102, 109, 122
 and religion 32, 124–130, 157
 and sewing 75–76
 and sloyd training 67–68
 beginnings of 27–33
 buildings of 47–56, 154–163
 criteria for admission 19, 161
 description of site xii, 21
 enactment of 14–16
 initial construction, 1900 22–26, 47, 56
 inmate's gift to 12
 machine shop of 78–79
 music program of 17, 53, 78, 98–105, 144, 154
 notable boys of 27, 32, 34, 37, 38, 39, 40, 59, 61, 139
 print shop of 64–66
 sheet metal shop of 78
 transition to Roebuck AYS campus 155
Alabama Building 52. See also Johnston Hall
Alabama Department of Youth Services xiii, 154–163, 168
 Chalkville campus (for girls) 154, 168
 Mt. Meigs campus 19, 155
 Roebuck campus 155
 Vacca campus xiv, 157–163
Alabama Federation of Women's Clubs ix, 12, 13, 17, 43
Alabama Industrial School for Negro Children xiii, 19, 155

Index

Alabama Juvenile Code 18–20, 165
Alabama National Guard 94, 96
Alabama Sheriffs' Boys' Ranches 169
Alabama State Penitentiary 165–166
Allgood, Myralyn xi
Annual Military Day 95, 96
Archibald 59
Arkansas 102
Armor, Judy xiv
Armor, Mrs. Curtis xiv
Athens State University xii, xiv
Auburn University x
Avery, Mary Johnston xiv, 4, 8, 13

B

Babcock, Maltbie 125
Baker, Mr. (ABIS teacher) 111
Bass, Sonny xiv
Berkshire Industrial Farm 13
Better Business Bureau 103
Bingham, Robert 7
Birmingham Age-Herald 66, 147
Birmingham, Alabama 10, 15, 19, 21, 24, 28, 34, 40, 43, 80, 105, 125, 134, 137, 157
Birmingham Building 48
Birmingham National Bank 10
Birmingham News 66, 84, 105, 121, 134, 151
Birmingham Post-Herald 57, 151
Birmingham Printing and Publishing xiii
Birmingham Public Library xiii
Birmingham-Southern College 102, 109, 154
Boy's Banner 64, 65, 107–115, 117, 119, 121, 123, 145, 146, 169
Branham, T. W. 110, 111
Brockway, Zebulon 98
Bush Chapel 54, 126, 156, 158
Bush, Mrs. T. G. 17, 18, 54, 126

C

Cadmean Circle 10
Caine, Cecil, Jr. xi
Calhoun Community College xii
Carr, John H. 89, 126, 154
Charlotte, North Carolina 8–9, 10, 146
Chester 38
Child Savers 165
Civil War 7, 166
Cobb, Sue Bell 170
Cole, Edmund W. 42
Cole, Mrs. S. D. 17, 27, 30
Commercial Club 22
Confederacy 7
Connelley, William 41
Converse, Mrs. James G. 17
convict leasing ix, 11
Cordova High School 122
Craighead Hall 54
Craighead, Mrs. Erwin 17, 54
criminal justice xii

D

Dawsey, James xiv, 36, 68, 69–71
Dawsey, Scott xiv, 70
Dix, Dorothea 166

E

Eager, Mrs. George B. 12, 13, 17, 31
East Lake 28, 32, 34, 45, 72, 105, 109, 118, 119, 125, 135
East Lake Park 144
Elmira Reformatory 98
Embree, John 28, 37, 38, 40
Epiphany Ministries 157
Ernest 37, 38
Evans, Elizabeth Johnson "Johnsie" 3–7. *See also* Johnston, Elizabeth Evans
Evans, Lizzie Morehead 3–4, 7
Evans, Peter 3, 5–7

F
Feagin, Judge 32
First Methodist Church (Birmingham) 103
Fitzpatrick, Mrs. E. S. 17
Flynt, Wayne ix–x, xi, xiv

G
George Junior Republic 13
Georgia 167
Gilmer, Harry 109–110
Government Printing Office 66
Graves, Bibb 66
Graves Hall 156
Green, Mr. (ABIS teacher) 89
Griffin, C. D. xii, xiii, 27–41, 47, 57, 64, 66, 73, 80, 86, 91, 98–99, 100, 107, 125, 144, 161
  hired as superintendent 27
  resignation as superintendent 40–41
Griffin, Mrs. C. D. 57, 98

H
Hall, J. D. 41, 42–43
Hart, Hastings Hornell 80, 85
Henderson, John D. 100–102
Henley, Arthur xiii
Hewitt High School 119
Highland Book Club 10, 55
Hill Hall 154
Hill, J. B. 154
House of Refuge 52, 164
Howard College 102, 109. *See also* Samford University

I
Ice Cream Manufacturer's Convention 103
Illinois 103
Italians 31

J
Jackson, F. M. 99
Jimmie 27, 29, 30–31, 32, 33, 34, 37, 144–145
Joe 61
Johnston Administration Building 162
Johnston Building 48
Johnston, Elizabeth Evans. *See also* Evans, Elizabeth Johnson "Johnsie"
  and hearing loss 8
  and hospital building 9
  and religious faith 3, 4, 9, 10–15, 21, 24–26, 43, 45, 46, 124, 128, 129, 130
  as ABIS president 17, 27, 29, 32, 34, 35, 42, 47, 57, 63, 71, 93, 102, 131, 132, 150, 164, 165, 167–170
  background of ix
  biography of xii, 166
  childhood of 3–7, 8
  death of 146–149
  literary interests of 10
  marriage of 8
Johnston, Evans 146
Johnston, Gordon 10, 13
Johnston Hall 52, 134. *See also* Alabama Building
Johnston, Joseph 10
Johnston, Louise 9
Johnston, Robert Douglas 6, 8, 10, 11
Jordan, Eugene C. 102, 103
juvenile delinquency 18, 19, 157
  contemporary challenges 168–170

K
Keith Vaudeville Circuit 102
Kilby Hall 77
Kilby, Thomas 66
Killough, J. N. 131, 133, 134, 137–138
Kilvington, William 42
Kruger, Ray 122

L

Legion Field 109
LeHigh Cement Company 103
Lingo, Mr. (ABIS teacher) 111
Lions Club 102
Little Mount Vernon 55, 146, 150

M

Marbury, Alabama 24
Massachusetts 166
Mercy Home 30
Montgomery 103
Montgomery Advertiser 105
Moore, B. F. 72
Morgantown, N.C. 7
Morris, Mr. (lumber donor) 23
Mr. Meade (court clerk) 32
Mt. Meigs, Alabama xiii, 19, 155, 168. *See also* Alabama Department of Youth Services: Mt. Meigs campus
Murray, George 30

N

Naval Reserve Band 103
New Boy Platoon 94
New York 5, 8, 13, 52, 98, 164
North Carolina 3, 7, 8, 104, 146
Nunnally, Mr. (ABIS teacher) 109, 121

O

Old Soldiers Reunion 103
Old South 3
Open Door System 41, 58

P

Parker (ABIS teamster) 30
Peabody College 42, 87
Peaton, Allen xiv
Porter, Benjamin F. 165
Pratt Coal Company ix
Pratt Mines 11
Progressive Era 165, 166

Protestant Women of Birmingham 168

R

Ramsey, Mrs. 30
Reconstruction 167
Red Mountain 37
Reformatory School. *See* Alabama Department of Youth Services: Mt. Meigs campus
reformers ix, 164–167
Rescue Home 168
Rickwood Field 102
Roosevelt, Theodore 13, 102
Ruhama Baptist Church 102

S

Saginaw, Alabama 22, 23
Samford University x, xi, xiv, 109. *See also* Howard College
Seale, Mr. (ABIS teacher) 111
segregation xiii, 19, 155, 167
Selma, Alabama 12
She Heard with Her Heart 8
Shelton, Bob 109
Shop Building 53
64th North Carolina Cavalry 7
slavery 3–4, 5, 165
Smith, Bobby 169
Smith, Don 74
Smith Hall 159, 160
Sousa, John Philip 98, 103, 105
South Highland Presbyterian Church 10, 146
Sparks, Chauncey 56, 93
Spurgeon 34–37, 39, 40
Stamps, Katherine 42, 89. *See also* Weakley, Katherine
State Federation of Colored Women's Clubs 168
State Training School for Girls 168. *See also* Alabama Department of Youth Services: Chalkville campus (for girls)

at Chalkville 168
Steiner Brothers Bank 25
Steiner, Burghard 25

T

Tarrant City 103
Taul, C. M. 81, 82
Teacher's Institute 29
Tennessee 13, 42, 43, 102, 151
Tennessee Coal and Iron Company 41
Tennessee Industrial School 42
Texas 102
Thomas, James xiv, 158
Trucks, Virgil 109–110
Tulane University 154
Turner, Carolyn 162
Tutwiler Hotel 103

U

Underwood, Oscar 93
University of Alabama xi, xii
U.S. Marine Band 102

V

Vacca, Pat 157
Virginia 7, 10, 55
vocational education 17, 42, 155

W

Wadsworth lumberyard 24
Walden, Joe 84
WAPI Radio 102
Washington, D.C. 102
Washington, George 55
Weakley, David xii, xiii, 41, 42–46,
    49–51, 54, 58–62, 64–66, 67–68,
    71, 72, 73, 78, 79, 83, 93, 96,
    99–100, 104, 117, 125, 129, 132,
    133, 136, 138, 139, 140, 143, 144,
    147, 163, 164, 167–170
  and education 67–68, 75, 79,
    82–83, 87–88, 90, 158
  and methods of care 58, 61
  hired as superintendent 43–44
  retirement of 149–153, 157
Weakley Hall 55, 56
Weakley, Katherine 43, 46, 87, 132,
    143, 149–153. *See also* Stamps,
    Katherine
Weakley, Mary Fryer 133
Weakley-Underwood Hall 159, 160
Williams, Owen 109
Windy 139
women's suffrage 16
Wood, H. C. 79, 94
Works Progress Administration 54
World War I 103, 145

www.ingramcontent.com/pod-product-compliance
Lightning Source LLC
Chambersburg PA
CBHW060341170426
43202CB00014B/2837